Fifty 400-Word Passages with Questions for Building Reading Speed

Timed
Readings
Level 1

Edward Spargo
Glenn R. Williston

Jamestown Publishers
Providence, R.I.

Timed Readings
No. TR-1 Level 1

ISBN 0-89061-031-2

Cover Design by
Stephen R. Anthony

᳨ Cover Photo by
Bob Emerson

Illustrations by
Mary M. Macdonald

Printed in the United States

CONTENTS

HOW TO USE THIS BOOK

1. Study and learn the Steps to Faster Reading on pages 9, 10, 11 and 12.

2. Turn to the selection to be read.

3. Wait for instructor's signal to begin.

4. Preview. (Allow 30 to 45 seconds if instructor does not time.)

5. Read selection, applying the remaining Steps to Faster Reading.

6. Note your reading time in minutes and seconds and jot it down.

7. Turn the page and answer the comprehension questions.

8. Correct your answers using the key on page 116 and 117.

9. Convert your reading time to a words-per-minute rate using the conversion table on page 120.

10. Enter your comprehension score and plot your reading rate on the graph on page 118 or 119.

INTRODUCTION

The eight-book series, *Timed Readings,* is designed to provide plentiful practice in building reading speed—and comprehension—using graded selections of standard word length.

The Reading Selections

For any drill to be productive and meaningful, all the elements of the practice, except one, should be held constant. In *Timed Readings* the selections in all eight books are 400 words long and all deal with factual information.

The variable element in the series is the reading level of the selections. Starting at grade six, each book advances one grade level, ending at college level. Readability of the selections was assessed by applying the Fry formula, using two samples within each selection.

Placement in the Series

To become a faster reader using *Timed Readings,* the learner must begin at an easy reading level. She can then progress to higher levels of difficulty while maintaining her improved reading rate. For most learners, this means starting at level 1.

How Fast Is Fast?

What is the optimum rate for each reader? Only the individual can determine the limit to which he can be challenged. Just as timing elicits exceptional performance from the athlete, the irrepressible impulse of the reader to beat the clock can produce spectacular progress.

For many students a rate of 400 words a minute would be impressive, if sustained, on factual material of the type included in *Timed Readings.* However, this rate should not be imposed as a standard for everyone, nor should it be allowed to become a ceiling for talented students.

Timing the Selections

For the instructor who wishes to help students time the selections, this method is suggested.

Write on the blackboard (or project using a transparency) these times:

:10	:20	:30	:40	:50	1:00
1:10	1:20	1:30	1:40	1:50	2:00
2:10	2:20	2:30	2:40	2:50	3:00
3:10	3:20	3:30	3:40	3:50	4:00
4:10	4:20	4:30	4:40	4:50	5:00

Give students the signal to preview; allow 30 to 45 seconds for this.

Direct students to read the selection and begin timing. At the end of ten seconds, erase *:10*; ten seconds later, erase *:20*; ten seconds later, erase *:30* and so on until all the numbers have been erased or all the students have finished reading.

Instruct students to look up to the board when they finish reading and copy the lowest time remaining (the next number to be erased).

Using this as their reading time, students can determine their words-per-minute rate from the table on page 120. Students timing themselves can use the time on the table closest to their actual reading time.

The Comprehension Questions

No achiever can claim success until he has been tested. In the case of *Timed Readings*, speed without comprehension is meaningless: the student must display adequate comprehension before his rate can be considered valid. Comprehension scores of 70 to 80 percent indicate that the learner is properly placed and comprehending satisfactorily.

The questions accompanying the selections were constructed with a single purpose mind—to demonstrate that the reader has, in fact, read the selection. In this regard, the questions may be considered comprehension checks rather than comprehension tests. A mix of question types—five fact and five thought questions—accompanies each selection.

An answer key on pages 116 and 117 permits immediate correction of responses and reinforcement of learning.

The Progress Graphs

Industry has discovered the usefulness of charts and graphs for employee motivation. The graphs on pages 118 and 119 help the student visualize her progress and reinforce her incentive to progress further.

Encourage students to maintain comprehension scores of 70 to 80 percent while gradually building reading rate.

Advancement to Successive Levels

A student who has reached a peak of reading speed (with satisfactory comprehension) is ready to advance to the next level in the *Timed Reading* series.

For example, a student who is reading regularly at 400 words a minute might better be challenged to maintain this rate on a higher and more difficult level in the series.

Students who can be encouraged to complete all fifty selections before moving on will have an excellent opportunity to consolidate their achievement.

STEP 1: PREVIEW

When you read, do you start in with the first word, or do you look over the whole selection for a moment? Good readers preview the selection first—this helps to make them good, and fast, readers.

How to Preview

1. **Read the Title.** The first thing to do when previewing is to read the title of the selection. Titles are designed not only to announce the subject, but also to make the reader think. What can you learn from the title? What thoughts does it bring to mind? What do you already know about this subject?

2. **Read the Opening Paragraph.** If the first paragraph is long, read the first sentence or two instead. The first paragraph is the writer's opportunity to greet the reader. He may have something to tell you about what is to come. Some writers announce what they hope to tell you in the selection. Some writers tell why they are writing. Some writers just try to get the reader's attention—they may ask a provocative question.

3. **Read the Closing Paragraph.** If the last paragraph is long, read just the final line or two. The closing paragraph is the writer's last chance to talk to his reader. He may have something important to say at the end. Some writers repeat the main idea once more. Some writers draw a conclusion: this is what they have been leading up to. Some writers summarize their thoughts; they tie all the facts together.

4. **Glance through.** Scan the selection quickly to see what else you can pick up. Discover whatever you can to help you read the selection. Are there names, dates, numbers? If so, you may have to read more slowly. Are there colorful adjectives? The selection might be light and fairly easy to read. Is the selection informative, containing a lot of facts, or conversational, an informal discussion with the reader?

STEP 2: READ FOR MEANING

When you read, do you just see words? Are you so occupied reading words that you sometimes fail to get the meaning? Good readers see beyond the words—they read for meaning. This makes them faster readers.

How to Read for Meaning

1. Build Concentration. You cannot read with understanding if you are not concentrating. Every reader's mind wanders occasionally; it is not a cause for alarm. When you discover that your thoughts have strayed, correct the situation right away. The longer you wait, the harder it becomes. Avoid distractions and distracting situations. Outside noises and activities will compete for your attention if you let them. Keep the preview information in mind as you read. This will help to focus your attention on the selection.

2. Read in Thought Groups. Individual words do not tell us much. They must be combined with other words in order to yield meaning. To obtain meaning from the printed page, therefore, the reader should see the words in meaningful combinations. If you see only a word at a time (called word-by-word reading), your comprehension suffers along with your speed. To improve both speed and comprehension, try to group the words into phrases which have a natural relationship to each other. For practice, you might want to read aloud, trying to speak the words in meaningful combinations.

3. Question the Author. To sustain the pace you have set for yourself, and to maintain a high level of comprehension, question the writer as you read. Continually ask yourself such questions as, "What does this mean? What is he saying now? How can I use this information?" Questions like these help you to concentrate fully on the selection.

STEP 3: GRASP PARAGRAPH SENSE

The paragraph is the basic unit of meaning. If you can discover quickly and understand the main point of each paragraph, you can comprehend the author's message. Good readers know how to find the main ideas of paragraphs quickly. This helps to make them fast readers.

How to Grasp Paragraph Sense

1. Find the Topic Sentence. The topic sentence, the sentence containing the main idea, is often the first sentence of a paragraph. It is followed by other sentences which support, develop, or explain the main idea. Sometimes a topic sentence comes at the end of a paragraph. When it does, the supporting details come first, building the base for the topic sentence. Some paragraphs do not have a topic sentence. Such paragraphs usually create a mood or feeling, rather than present information.

2. Understand Paragraph Structure. Every well-written paragraph has purpose. The purpose may be to inform, define, explain, persuade, compare or contrast, illustrate, and so on. The purpose should always relate to the main idea and expand on it. As you read each paragraph, see how the body of the paragraph is used to tell you more about the main idea or topic sentence. Read the supporting details intelligently, recognizing that what you are reading is all designed to develop the single main idea.

STEP 4: ORGANIZE FACTS

how does it all fit ?

When you read, do you tend to see a lot of facts without any apparent connection or relationship? Understanding how the facts all fit together to deliver the author's message is, after all, the reason for reading. Good readers organize facts as they read. This helps them to read rapidly and well.

How to Organize Facts

1. Discover the Writer's Plan. Look for a clue or signal word early in the article which might reveal the author's structure. Every writer has a plan or outline which he follows. If the reader can discover his method of organization, he has the key to understanding the message. Sometimes the author gives you obvious signals. If he says, "There are three reasons. . ." the wise reader looks for a listing of the three items. Other less obvious signal words such as *moreover, otherwise, consequently* all tell the reader the direction the writer's message will take.

2. Relate as You Read. As you read the selection, keep the information learned during the preview in mind. See how the ideas you are reading all fit into place. Consciously strive to relate what you are reading to the title. See how the author is carrying through in his attempt to piece together a meaningful message. As you discover the relationship among the ideas, the message comes through quickly and clearly.

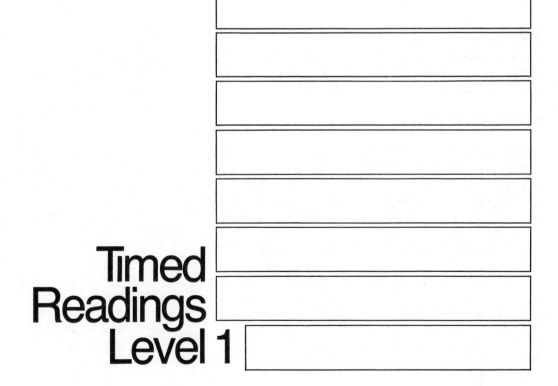

Timed
Readings
Level 1

1. COINS IN OUR LIVES

Every day of our lives we use coins in many different ways. We use them in candy machines and telephone booths, on the bus and in the store. We use coins to buy stamps, food, and all the little things that make our lives more comfortable.

Aside from allowing us to buy things with them, coins are an important reminder of our national heritage. They tell about the liberties and freedoms we cherish. The symbols on them tell us of the long history of our country and of the work and sacrifices of our forefathers.

The American colonists suffered under the burden of having to use many different types of coins from England, Spain, France, Holland and Germany. The mixture of these coins was confusing because they did not all have the same value. After the American Revolution, one of the first duties of the new leaders of the United States was to create coins. A law was passed by Congress in 1792 providing for a national coinage and the establishment of a United States Mint to make coins. The first official Mint was located in Philadelphia, where copper cents and half cents were first made for public use.

Other laws permitted the building of Mints in different cities throughout the country and also allowed the government to establish the Bureau of the Mint as part of the United States Treasury Department. The headquarters of both the Mint and the Treasury are in our nation's capital. Today there are three Mints that produce our national coinage. They are located at Philadelphia, Denver, and San Francisco. The Philadelphia and Denver Mints are open daily for visitors.

Coins are round so they won't wear holes in people's pockets. Centuries ago, coins were carried in pouches with a draw-string around the mouth of the bag. The same string allowed people to tie the moneybag to their belts when clothing didn't have a lot of pockets and women didn't carry purses. Another reason coins are round is that round coins are easier to use in vending machines.

The sizes of our coins today are decided by law, but they generally follow a tradition set by the ancient Greeks and Romans. It is necessary for coins to be a convenient size, not too small to be easily lost or overlooked, and not so large they are uncomfortable or difficult to use and carry.

Selection 1: Recalling Facts

1. The colonists used coins from
   ☐ a. Denmark.   ☐ b. Portugal.   ☐ c. Holland.

2. The United States Mint was established in the early
   ☐ a. 1790s.   ☐ b. 1820s.   ☐ c. 1830s.

3. The first official mint was located in
   ☐ a. New York.   ☐ b. San Francisco.   ☐ c. Philadelphia.

4. The first coins were made of
   ☐ a. silver.   ☐ b. gold.   ☐ c. copper.

5. Today, one U.S. Mint is located in
   ☐ a. Denver.   ☐ b. Chicago.   ☐ c. Boston.

Selection 1: Understanding Ideas

6. Coins are round so that
   ☐ a. they can be stacked in even piles.
   ☐ b. they will not damage clothing.
   ☐ c. they will take less space in bank vaults.

7. The sizes of American coins are like those used by
   ☐ a. ancient Oriental civilizations.
   ☐ b. early European peoples.
   ☐ c. South American governments.

8. The author implies that a study of coinage reveals
   ☐ a. trends in clothing fashions over the years.
   ☐ b. the history of American expansion.
   ☐ c. people's preferences for certain metals.

9. Most of this selection is concerned with
   ☐ a. laws governing the use of coins.
   ☐ b. the process of minting coins.
   ☐ c. the history of coins.

10. We can conclude that American coins
    ☐ a. are easy to handle.
    ☐ b. are the most popular in the world.
    ☐ c. show historic events.

16

2. A NEW WAY OF LIFE

The history of our form of government begins with its settlers. Most of the early settlers came from England. They lived in groups called colonies. The King of England was their ruler.

The English settlers founded the Virginia colony at Jamestown in 1607. It was the first permanent English colony. In 1620 other English people came to America. They were known as Pilgrims. They went to Holland first. In Holland, their children began to forget the English ways. They decided to leave Holland and go to the New World. They founded Plymouth colony in Massachusetts. They struggled to build homes and to exist. After a hard winter, the Pilgrims who survived held a feast with the Indians who had helped them begin their new way of life. They thanked God for their blessings. This was the first American Thanksgiving.

More Englishmen, as well as people from other European countries, came to live in America. Many, like the Pilgrims, wanted to be free to worship God in their own way. Others were looking for political freedom. Traders were seeking to make money. The poor and the unemployed people wanted jobs and the chance to earn a better living. Businessmen who had money to invest saw promise of success in America.

After many years, all of the colonists came under British rule. Georgia, founded in 1733, was the last colony to be formed. In 1776, there were thirteen British colonies in the part of America that later became the United States. These colonies became the first thirteen states.

The King let the colonists elect representatives to make local laws. The colonists were free in many ways. But, as time passed, more and more laws for the colonists were made in Great Britain. Under these laws, the colonists had to pay more taxes. However, the colonists were not asked to help make these laws. They had no spokesmen in Great Britain. They began to feel that some of their rights were being taken away from them. They said they could be taxed only by their own officials. The King refused to change the tax laws.

The colonists decided to hold a meeting to discuss their problems. All of the colonies except Georgia sent men to this meeting. It was held in Philadelphia in 1774. It was the First Continental Congress. They asked the King for their rights as Englishmen.

Selection 2: Recalling Facts

1. Most of the early settlers of the United States came from
   □ a. Germany. □ b. Denmark. □ c. England.

2. Jamestown, Virginia, was founded in the early
   □ a. 1500s. □ b. 1600s. □ c. 1700s.

3. Before the Pilgrims came to America, they lived in
   □ a. France. □ b. Scotland. □ c. Holland.

4. The last colony to be founded was
   □ a. Rhode Island. □ b. Georgia. □ c. Virginia.

5. The Continental Congress was held in
   □ a. Philadelphia. □ b. Boston. □ c. New York City.

Selection 2: Understanding Ideas

6. Most of the first people who came to America were seeking
   □ a. wealth and opportunity.
   □ b. religious freedom.
   □ c. better jobs.

7. The colonists turned against the King of England when
   □ a. they could not make their own money.
   □ b. they could not send representatives to England.
   □ c. they could not trade with other countries.

8. At the First Continental Congress, the officials did not hear
   □ a. any discussion of rights and freedoms.
   □ b. any talk about England.
   □ c. any speeches from Georgia delegates.

9. The Pilgrims came to America because
   □ a. their children were forgetting their English customs.
   □ b. they heard that the streets in America were paved with gold.
   □ c. the King of England would not allow them to stay in England.

10. We can conclude that
    □ a. people from many different countries lived in the colonies.
    □ b. the King of England was a weak ruler.
    □ c. early colonists wanted to break away from England.

3. TO TRAIN A CAT

Cats are clean animals and easy to housebreak. A shallow pan or box can be covered with an inch or so of sand, sawdust, or litter. Litter can be bought at pet stores, supermarkets, and hardware stores. The pan should always be in the same place.

To teach a cat, one must watch him carefully. When he begins to search for one place after another, he must be put into his pan. The litter must be changed often, and the pan must be washed with soap and water every few days.

A cat will scratch to wear off his old claws. He will need a scratching post to reduce damage to furniture. Every time the cat claws at the furniture, the scratching post should be pointed out to him until he learns to use it without help.

A cat enjoys a soft ball, a toy mouse, or some other kind of toy. Such objects should be too large for the cat to swallow.

Most cats enjoy playing. They are independent animals, however, and play only when they feel like it.

Most cats refuse to be disciplined although they may understand "no." They learn their names quickly, and many will come when called. If a cat is told what to do and he likes the trick, he will learn to do it.

A cat should be confined to the house, especially at night. Cats that are allowed to roam disturb the neighbors with their crying and fighting. A female cat should never be allowed to roam during her mating season.

Proper care usually will eliminate the threat of disease or injury. Unusual symptoms should be watched for, and visits to the veterinarian should be regular. A cat must be vaccinated early against rabies and other serious diseases.

A cat will lick his fur to clean it. As he licks it, he will swallow hairs that form little felt-like balls in his stomach and intestines.

Although hair balls can be prevented by brushing a cat daily, some will form anyway. A veterinarian can prescribe a remedy to help a cat eliminate the hair.

A cat should never be dropped because he can be seriously injured. Cats do not always land on their feet as many people think.

Selection 3: Recalling Facts

1. A cat's litter box must be washed with soap and water
   ☐ a. every few days.   ☐ b. once a week.   ☐ c. once a month.

2. A cat scratches objects
   ☐ a. to sharpen his claws.
   ☐ b. to wear down his claws.
   ☐ c. to exercise.

3. Cats should not be given playthings that are
   ☐ a. too small.   ☐ b. too large.   ☐ c. too rough.

4. The author says that cats are
   ☐ a. proud.   ☐ b. quick.   ☐ c. independent.

5. Cats should be vaccinated to prevent
   ☐ a. rabies.   ☐ b. heartworm.   ☐ c. distemper.

Selection 3: Understanding Ideas

6. A cat will learn a trick
   ☐ a. if he is fed immediately before the trick.
   ☐ b. if he is scolded when he fails to do the trick.
   ☐ c. if he enjoys what he is doing.

7. To housebreak a cat, the owner should
   ☐ a. change the litter in the box every few hours.
   ☐ b. keep the litter box in the same place.
   ☐ c. reward the cat if he uses the litter box.

8. Cats should be kept indoors at night because
   ☐ a. they are noisy.
   ☐ b. they may catch cold.
   ☐ c. they may run away.

9. A veterinarian is
   ☐ a. a pet store owner.
   ☐ b. an animal trainer.
   ☐ c. an animal doctor.

10. We can conclude that
    ☐ a. cats are very difficult to housebreak.
    ☐ b. cats are intelligent and easy to train.
    ☐ c. cats require a minimum of care.

4. THE NEEDS OF THE PEOPLE

The Constitution has been changed to serve the needs of the people. When it was accepted in 1789, there were no large cities. There were no railroads and very few factories. Most of the people lived on farms. Today, most people live in cities. Their lives are tied together. Our government had to serve new needs of the nation as they arose. How was this done?

The Constitution has developed through general laws. The Congress, the President, and the courts have needed help to carry out their duties. Boards have been set up to study the needs of the people and to advise the Congress of changes that should be made in the laws. The Congress has set up other government boards and offices with authority to make rules.

The Congress has passed laws giving the President more departments in his Cabinet. In 1789, there were only four departments. Today there are eleven departments. The Congress has added new federal courts as they have been needed. By these and other general laws, the Congress has helped to organize the government under the Constitution. The government has been changed to meet the new needs of the people.

The Constitution has developed also through treaties. The United States must get along well with other nations. We trade with people in many lands. The ships of other nations often carry our goods. Our citizens travel, live, and die in other countries. The citizens of other nations live and trade here.

The writers of the Constitution did not know what matters should be covered by treaties. They decided to let the President and the Senate develop this part of the Constitution. They declared in Article II that the President "shall have power, by and with the advice and consent of the Senate, to make treaties, provided two-thirds of the senators present concur."

The Constitution does not say when or on what subjects treaties shall be made. These matters are left to the President and to the Senate. For example, the Constitution does not say whether citizens of other countries can own land in the United States. But the President and the Senate have made treaties with other nations giving their citizens the right to own land in the United States. Texas came into the Union by a treaty with the United States. These are two examples that show how treaties help to give life to the Constitution.

Selection 4: Recalling Facts

1. The Constitution was written in
   - ☐ a. 1776.
   - ☐ b. 1789.
   - ☐ c. 1823.

2. The greatest number of people today live in
   - ☐ a. cities.
   - ☐ b. towns.
   - ☐ c. rural areas.

3. How many departments did the first United States Cabinet have?
   - ☐ a. Three
   - ☐ b. Four
   - ☐ c. Five

4. What state came into the Union by a treaty?
   - ☐ a. Arizona
   - ☐ b. Texas
   - ☐ c. Georgia

5. To help carry out its duties, the Congress sets up
   - ☐ a. departments.
   - ☐ b. boards.
   - ☐ c. courts.

Selection 4: Understanding Ideas

6. According to the article,
   - ☐ a. the Constitution has been rewritten.
   - ☐ b. the government has been changed.
   - ☐ c. the role of the President has been changed.

7. The Constitution is able to meet the changing needs of the people through
   - ☐ a. treaties.
   - ☐ b. declarations.
   - ☐ c. popular votes.

8. The author uses "treaty" to mean
   - ☐ a. law.
   - ☐ b. agreement.
   - ☐ c. power.

9. Article II of the Constitution deals with
   - ☐ a. Presidential power.
   - ☐ b. foreign countries.
   - ☐ c. trade agreements.

10. The author states that Congress
    - ☐ a. makes laws.
    - ☐ b. enforces laws.
    - ☐ c. breaks laws.

5. GRADING OF EGGS

The U.S. Department of Agriculture requires that a grade mark be used on eggs. It is printed on the carton or on a tape used to seal the carton. It shows both the grade and the size of the eggs. Sometimes the size is not printed in the grade mark but is printed on the carton.

There are three grades for eggs. The top grade is U.S. Grade AA, or Fresh Fancy Quality. The next is U.S. Grade A. U.S. Grade B is the lowest grade.

Some stores sell all three grades, and there may be quite a difference in price between the grades.

The top two grades, AA and A, are best for frying and poaching. They don't spread out very much in the pan, and the yolk is firm and not easily broken.

Grade B eggs are just as good to eat. But the white is thinner. Also, the yolk may be flatter than in eggs of the higher grades.

In most states, eggs marked with a grade and size must meet state laws. Many state grade standards are the same as those of the U.S.

Eggs come in different sizes. But the size has nothing to do with the quality. So you have two decisions to make in buying eggs—the grade and the size.

A dozen Small eggs must weigh at least 18 ounces. Mediums must weigh at least 21 ounces. Large eggs must weigh at least 24 ounces. As you can see, there is a 3-ounce difference between each size.

Smaller eggs sell for less than the bigger ones because you really buy them by weight just as you do meat and other foods.

For example, let's say Large Grade A eggs are selling for 80 cents a dozen. To be of equal value, a dozen Medium Grade A eggs would sell for about 7 cents less, or 73 cents. Small Grade A eggs would sell for 7 cents less than the Mediums, or 66 cents. If the smaller sizes were priced much below this, you could get more for your money by buying the smaller sizes.

A buyer should watch for bargains in these smaller-sized eggs in late summer and fall when they're plentiful. If a person makes it a habit to check the price difference between sizes, then he'll be able to spot the bargains when they're available.

Selection 5: Recalling Facts

1. Which federal department requires grade marks on eggs?
   - ☐ a. Commerce
   - ☐ b. Interior
   - ☐ c. Agriculture

2. Grade marks indicate
   - ☐ a. size and quality.
   - ☐ b. color and texture.
   - ☐ c. price and shape.

3. The lowest grade allowed for eggs is
   - ☐ a. Grade B.
   - ☐ b. Grade C.
   - ☐ c. Grade D.

4. Grading marks are usually located on
   - ☐ a. the eggs.
   - ☐ b. the carton.
   - ☐ c. the tag.

5. What is the weight difference between each size of eggs?
   - ☐ a. 2 ounces
   - ☐ b. 3 ounces
   - ☐ c. 4 ounces

Selection 5: Understanding Ideas

6. Some states label eggs Jumbo.
   - ☐ a. This labeling is not legal.
   - ☐ b. These eggs would be larger than Large.
   - ☐ c. No one would be able to afford these eggs.

7. A person who wishes to use eggs for baking a cake should buy
   - ☐ a. Grade AA, Medium.
   - ☐ b. Grade A, Large.
   - ☐ c. Grade B, Medium.

8. Which one of the following should be the most inexpensive?
   - ☐ a. Grade AA, Medium
   - ☐ b. Grade A, Large
   - ☐ c. Grade B, Medium

9. U.S. Grade A eggs
   - ☐ a. have firm yolks.
   - ☐ b. are often smaller than other grades.
   - ☐ c. have thinner shells.

10. We can conclude that
    - ☐ a. supermarkets offer the lowest egg prices.
    - ☐ b. grade does not necessarily indicate price.
    - ☐ c. Medium and Large eggs are priced lower in winter.

6. TEA AND TAXES

The cost of a war is always high. The British had had to fight France both in Europe and in America. Great Britain needed more money.

The King thought that the colonists were using goods on which taxes had not been paid. He ordered his officers to search for such goods without giving any reasons.

The colonists were not pleased. They were Englishmen. They said that they could not be searched unless the officer gave them a written statement telling why the search was made. But the officers took orders from the King and refused to listen to the colonists.

For many years the King and the Parliament had taxed goods that were brought into the colonies from other countries. Great Britain wanted the colonies to trade with her. She had told the colonists what goods they could make and with whom they could trade. But Great Britain had not placed heavy taxes on the colonists. She had not asked that the colonists give much money to support the mother country.

Following the war with France, Great Britain kept an army of soldiers in the colonies. The King, George III, decided that the colonists should pay the cost of the army. So the Parliament passed a new tax law. It forced the colonists to buy tax stamps and to put them on newspapers, deeds, and all business papers. The colonists could neither buy nor sell anything without paying the new taxes.

The colonists were not against taxes. But they did not like to be taxed against their wishes. They did not have representatives in the Parliament. They said that it was wrong to force the colonists to pay the taxes. It was against their rights as Englishmen. For a hundred years, all Englishmen had said that they could be taxed only by their own representatives.

At first King George III and the Parliament refused to change the tax laws. Many of the colonists would not buy the tax stamps. Some of the people took the stamps and burned them. At last, the friends of the colonists in the Parliament had the tax laws changed.

The Parliament then put a tax on all paint, paper, glass, lead, and tea that were brought into the colonies. Again, the colonists did not like the new taxes. They refused to buy any goods from Great Britain until the tax laws were changed.

Selection 6: Recalling Facts

1. The English government taxed
   □ a. tobacco.   □ b. paint.   □ c. coffee.

2. The colonists did not mind being searched if the officers
   □ a. were French.   □ b. paid a tax.   □ c. had search papers.

3. The King mentioned in the article is
   □ a. George III.   □ b. Henry VIII.   □ c. Edward I.

4. Tax stamps were used on
   □ a. cigarettes.   □ b. letters.   □ c. newspapers.

5. Most of the colonists were
   □ a. French.   □ b. English.   □ c. German.

Selection 6: Understanding Ideas

6. England taxed goods shipped to the colonies from other countries
   □ a. because England wanted all the trade.
   □ b. because goods from foreign countries were not well made.
   □ c. because England wanted a war with the colonies.

7. According to the article, the stamp tax
   □ a. was a great success for many years.
   □ b. was ignored by the colonists.
   □ c. was a complete failure.

8. This article is mostly concerned with
   □ a. the cost of war.
   □ b. the English government.
   □ c. British power in the colonies.

9. The author states that the colonists
   □ a. hated all taxes.
   □ b. would not pay a tax to vote in elections.
   □ c. wanted to be taxed by their own officials.

10. Early colonists were unable to make
    □ a. pewter.   □ b. paper.   □ c. pans.

7. BEAKS AND BILLS

When one thinks of birds and their mouths, many different types come to mind. An observer might wonder why they are all so different.

Unlike humans who have hands and tools to prepare their foods to fit their mouths, birds must have mouths to fit their foods. A person might study a few different types of birds, the shapes of their mouths, and the types of food they eat.

Having a backyard feeder allows one to be most familiar with the seed eaters. They have short, stout bills that are well suited for cracking hard seed coats to expose the tender kernels. The sharp tip of the beak is useful for capturing insects, which are also part of their diet.

Insects play a large part in the diet of many birds. Insect eaters have thin bills that allow them to remove insects and insect eggs from in and among the leaves and pieces of bark.

There are also flying insect eaters. Although these birds have tiny, weak beaks, their mouths open wide like traps to scoop up insects in flight. Purple martins, members of the swallow family, are well known for their insect-eating abilities. People often build martin houses to attract them.

Woodpeckers have hard bills with which they hollow out their nests and bore for grubs in tree bark. Woodpeckers have long bills and, like hummingbirds, they are the only birds with tongues that can extend beyond the tips of their bills to help in food gathering. Once the hole has been bored and the insect is found, the woodpecker sticks his pointed tongue into the hole to pull out the insect.

Since the hummingbird's food is the sweet nectar found deep within flower blossoms, nature has given this bird a long, thin bill for searching deep into flowers. The long tongue, like a tube, can extend beyond the tip of the bill. It can reach into the deepest blossom to suck the nectar. Tiny insects inside the flowers also are eaten. Changes within the species have caused some hummingbirds to have either longer or shorter bills. Some have bills that are straight, curve up, or curve down to fit more easily into flowers that are common in an area.

Birds of prey, such as eagles, owls, hawks, and falcons have sharp-edged, hooked bills that are used to tear bite-sized pieces of flesh from the animals they capture and kill.

Selection 7: Recalling Facts

1. Birds' mouths are shaped according to
   - ☐ a. the food they eat.
   - ☐ b. their place of birth.
   - ☐ c. the way they fight.

2. The bills of seed eaters are
   - ☐ a. long.
   - ☐ b. blunt.
   - ☐ c. short.

3. Seed-eating birds also may eat
   - ☐ a. worms.
   - ☐ b. insects.
   - ☐ c. plants.

4. Insect eggs are often found
   - ☐ a. behind bark.
   - ☐ b. in grasses.
   - ☐ c. on buildings.

5. Purple martins belong to the
   - ☐ a. wren family.
   - ☐ b. swallow family.
   - ☐ c. sparrow family.

Selection 7: Understanding Ideas

6. Purple martins have
   - ☐ a. long, sharp beaks.
   - ☐ b. large mouths.
   - ☐ c. sharp claws.

7. Woodpeckers are like hummingbirds because they both
   - ☐ a. drink nectar.
   - ☐ b. use their sharp claws for defense.
   - ☐ c. have useful tongues.

8. Eagles are mentioned as examples of birds which
   - ☐ a. nest on high cliffs.
   - ☐ b. tear their food apart.
   - ☐ c. kill many farm animals each year.

9. People are most familiar with birds which have
   - ☐ a. short, stout beaks.
   - ☐ b. long, slender bills.
   - ☐ c. sharp-edged, hooked bills.

10. We can conclude that
    - ☐ a. hummingbirds show more variety in bill shape than any other bird.
    - ☐ b. people should feed birds during cold winter months.
    - ☐ c. eagles and falcons are becoming very rare.

8. RIGHTS OF ALIENS

An alien is a person who is not a citizen of this country. In the United States an alien has many, but not all, of the rights of a citizen.

An alien does not have the right to vote. He cannot hold public office or a government job. He cannot serve on a jury.

However, there are many rights that an alien can enjoy. For example, an alien is protected by the Constitution of the United States. The Constitution gives him the right to speak freely and the right to worship as he pleases. The alien also has the right to travel and to own property. He has the right to police and fire protection. And he has the right to an education for himself and his family.

Many federal, state, and local laws protect the alien. One of these laws protects the worker who has lost his job. The state pays him a certain amount of money until he can find a job. He may be paid for as long as 36 weeks in some states. The money to pay the worker comes from a special tax paid by the employer.

Anyone can become needy. A person may grow too old to work or become ill. Worst of all, he may die and leave the members of his family with no one to support them.

Many years ago, the federal government began a social security plan for workers. The plan insures working people against the loss of wages caused by old age, injury, illness, or death.

A worker earns his right to social security by paying a special tax. This tax is taken out of the wages he earns while working for someone else. If he works for himself, he pays a different kind of tax.

If a man works for someone else, his employer takes a few cents out of each dollar he earns. The employer takes the same amount of his money and sends it with the worker's money to the government. If a person works for himself, his tax is a little more than if he were working for someone else.

When a person grows old and cannot do much work, he may decide to stop working. Before he retires, he should consider how much money he will receive from social security. He may need it to help pay rent and buy food and clothing.

Selection 8: Recalling Facts

1. According to the author, an alien
   - ☐ a. is not a citizen.
   - ☐ b. has no rights.
   - ☐ c. cannot read or write.

2. An alien is not allowed
   - ☐ a. to own property.
   - ☐ b. to travel.
   - ☐ c. to vote.

3. Aliens are protected by
   - ☐ a. the Declaration of Independence.
   - ☐ b. the Constitution.
   - ☐ c. the Magna Carta.

4. In some states an alien who is not working can receive payment for
   - ☐ a. 10 weeks.
   - ☐ b. 36 weeks.
   - ☐ c. 52 weeks.

5. Social security was begun by the
   - ☐ a. employers.
   - ☐ b. state governments.
   - ☐ c. the federal government.

Selection 8: Understanding Ideas

6. Social security payments are made
   - ☐ a. by the worker when he files his income tax.
   - ☐ b. before the worker receives his wages.
   - ☐ c. by the worker twice a year.

7. When an alien becomes too old to work,
   - ☐ a. he must return to his native country.
   - ☐ b. he must enter a special home for the elderly.
   - ☐ c. he may apply for social security benefits.

8. The author implies that a worker
   - ☐ a. pays half of his total social security tax.
   - ☐ b. must be employed for ten years before he can collect benefits.
   - ☐ c. pays less social security tax if he works for himself.

9. We can assume that an alien
   - ☐ a. does not have to pay federal income tax.
   - ☐ b. must serve on a jury if he is called.
   - ☐ c. must be paid the same wages as a citizen.

10. An alien who wishes to practice the religion of his homeland
    - ☐ a. must first obtain permission from the federal government.
    - ☐ b. must file an application with his state government.
    - ☐ c. may do so without permission from anyone.

9. A BUCKET BRIGADE

In the dry heat of late summer, forty hikers, campers, and high-lake fishermen avoided disaster. With hands, sticks, and tin cookware, these men and women stopped and put out a fire on the steep north slope above middle Mildred Lake in Mason County.

It was the last holiday weekend of the summer. It was one last chance to take a high-lake fishing trip and to backpack with the family before school began again.

It was hot. There had been no rain for days, and the air was still. People were warned of the high fire danger and were urged to be extra cautious.

At six that Sunday evening, campers around the Mildred Lakes noticed smoke rising above the middle lake. Within minutes, flames were leaping into the air. Immediately, people were on the scene, anxious to do whatever possible to put out the blaze.

One of the fishermen, a Game Department employee, had worked as a smoke-jumper on fire crews in his youth. He organized the group to circle the blaze with trenches. The only hope was to form a fire line and to attempt to contain the blaze.

In an oval area of 75 yards, some of the fire fighters scraped the earth with whatever they had, while a number of girls formed a line to the lake, which was 100 yards downhill. The girls were sending buckets of water up the slope to the fire. The group worked as a team for nearly three hours. They dug trenches around the blaze and, at the same time, covered the flames with earth. By darkness, the flames had been smothered and the fire was under control.

While the fire was blazing, a Forest Service patrol aircraft had been seen overhead. Men from the Forest Service then reported the blaze. A standby fire crew was sent out and arrived late that night. The regular fire crew arrived early the next morning and remained on the scene for 72 hours, pumping water on the area and watching for any sign of further burning.

Fighting a fire is an activity unusual to the typical, high-lake fishing trip. It is something definitely not in the plans. But the concern, dedication, and hard work of the people involved is proof that American outdoorsmen are gifted with a common sense of responsibility. They do care about the environment.

Selection 9: Recalling Facts

1. The total number of campers, hikers, and fishermen mentioned is
   □ a. 20. □ b. 40. □ c. 60.

2. The events in the article occurred on
   □ a. Saturday. □ b. Sunday. □ c. Monday.

3. How long did the team work to put the fire out?
   □ a. Three hours □ b. Twelve hours □ c. Twenty-four hours

4. Volunteers controlled the fire with a bucket brigade and
   □ a. back-fires. □ b. hand pumps. □ c. trenches.

5. Buckets had to be passed a distance of
   □ a. 50 yards. □ b. 100 yards. □ c. 200 yards.

Selection 9: Understanding Ideas

6. The holiday mentioned in the article was
   □ a. Memorial Day. □ b. Fourth of July. □ c. Labor Day.

7. To put out the fire, campers used
   □ a. fire extinguishers they had brought with them.
   □ b. special fire blankets located along the trail.
   □ c. everything they could find close by.

8. The fire spread quickly because
   □ a. the forest was dry.
   □ b. the campers did not see the fire for some time.
   □ c. lightning struck in several separate places.

9. The author praises the work of
   □ a. the local fire-fighting company.
   □ b. the Civil Air Patrol.
   □ c. the campers.

10. From the information in the article we can assume that
    □ a. no one was injured fighting the fire.
    □ b. the fire continued to burn for nearly a week.
    □ c. the fire was started by a burning cigarette.

10. A LITTLE GRASS SHACK

On world maps the Caribbean islands are shown as being tropical. The economy of the region is based mainly on farming. Farmers are of two types. First is the plantation owner with his spread of hundreds or thousands of acres. The other type is the small cultivator working a few acres of land. Truck farming is done near some of the cities. On some farms families barely manage to get by on what they grow.

As in the early days, sugar is the main product. Other export crops are tobacco, coffee, bananas, citrus fruits and spices. From the West Indies also come oil, asphalt and many forest products. Jamaica's aluminum ore supplies are the world's largest. Oil comes from Trinidad, Aruba, and Curacao. But for many of the smaller islands, sugar is the only export.

Rum, which is distilled from sugar cane, is also an export. The world's best rum comes from this area. Local kinds vary from the light rums of Puerto Rico to the heavier, darker rums of Barbados and Jamaica. In Curacao the well-known liquor of that name is made from rinds of a special, native orange.

Ever since America's colonial days, the Caribbean islands have been favorite places to visit. Since World War II tourism has increased rapidly. Because great numbers of people go there, the islanders have built hotels, developed harbors and airfields, improved beaches, and have expanded sea and air routes.

As in any other part of the world, this area has differences in the ways in which the people live. Those who have money live well indeed. Those who don't have money live at various levels of poverty. The poor greatly outnumber the wealthy.

A visitor will find rich people living happily in cool, Spanish villas or modern homes and apartments. Their servants might include a cook, a maid, and a nurse for the children.

Most of the people are quite poor, with incomes of only a few hundred dollars, or even less. In the towns they live crowded together in rows of tiny houses. The houses are painted pretty colors when they can afford paint. In the countryside the poor live mainly in shacks or lean-tos that are put together in clever ways. Many poor people live in thatched-roof huts so typical of the tropics. Trees and flowering shrubs sometimes add an interesting background.

Selection 10: Recalling Facts

1. The Caribbean islands are
   ☐ a. temperate. ☐ b. semi-tropical. ☐ c. tropical.

2. The economy of the Caribbean islands is based on
   ☐ a. tourism. ☐ b. industry. ☐ c. farming.

3. Jamaica is the world's largest supplier of
   ☐ a. sugar. ☐ b. aluminum. ☐ c. tobacco.

4. Sugar cane can be distilled into
   ☐ a. rum. ☐ b. vinegar. ☐ c. molasses.

5. Most people on the islands are
   ☐ a. wealthy. ☐ b. middle class. ☐ c. poor.

Selection 10: Understanding Ideas

6. This article is primarily about
   ☐ a. industry in the West Indies.
   ☐ b. vacationing in the Caribbean.
   ☐ c. the economy of Caribbean islands.

7. The article states that
   ☐ a. even rich people in the West Indies cannot afford servants.
   ☐ b. farm land is owned by the government.
   ☐ c. several varieties of rum are made in the Caribbean.

8. We can conclude that sugar cane grows well in
   ☐ a. a tropical climate. ☐ b. an arid climate. ☐ c. a cool climate.

9. Ever since America's colonial days,
   ☐ a. the islands have been United States colonies.
   ☐ b. the Caribbean islands have welcomed tourists.
   ☐ c. the islands have wanted to become states.

10. The island of Curacao is famous for its
    ☐ a. wide, sandy beaches.
    ☐ b. beautiful gardens.
    ☐ c. orange-flavored liquor.

11. BUYING A LADDER

Ladders once were simple constructions of wood timbers and cross pieces, notched and bound with thongs. Today, the range of ladder designs, types, sizes and materials is broad enough to meet all needs.

Before one makes a trip to the store to buy a ladder, he should think about his needs. Will the ladder be used indoors or outdoors? How high will he want to climb? Who will be using it? Where will it be stored?

If he lives in an apartment, he will need a stepladder which will meet his needs and will be easy to handle. Its size will depend on the highest point he wants to reach. He should remember that he must never stand on the top of a stepladder.

A person who lives in a house may need two ladders, a stepladder for indoor work and a straight ladder or extension ladder for use outdoors. The outdoor ladder should be long enough to extend a minimum of three feet higher than the highest area he wants to reach.

A person who is buying a stepladder should never be hurried into making a quick purchase. The ladder should be checked for weak steps, loose rungs, or other weaknesses before it is taken from the store.

A buyer should check to see if the name of the manufacturer or distributor appears on the label. This information may be important in case of a quality or accident problem.

Wood, aluminum, magnesium and fiber glass are the principal materials used in the construction of modern ladders. Each type has its advantages and disadvantages.

Wood ladders are sturdy and bend little under loads for which they are designed. They are heavier than metal ladders, and large sizes are harder to handle. When dry, wood ladders are safe to use around electrical circuits or when a person is working with power tools.

Metal ladders are a little more expensive than wood ladders of the same quality. They last longer because they do not decay from moisture and sunlight and are not attacked by insects. Aluminum and magnesium ladders are light, weighing only about two-thirds as much as those made of wood.

Fiber glass is the newest material to appear on the ladder market. It is used to make the side rails of high-grade metal stepladders. The result is a ladder that is light, rust resistant, serviceable and practically carefree.

Selection 11: Recalling Facts

1. How far should outdoor ladders extend beyond the area to be reached?
   □ a. One foot   □ b. Two feet   □ c. Three feet

2. The heaviest ladders are made of
   □ a. fiberglass.   □ b. metal.   □ c. wood.

3. Ladders are sometimes made of a combination of fiberglass and
   □ a. aluminum.   □ b. wood.   □ c. plastic.

4. What type of ladder is not affected by moisture and sunlight?
   □ a. Wood   □ b. Aluminum   □ c. Fiberglass

5. If a ladder proves to be defective, the buyer should contact
   □ a. the police.
   □ b. the manufacturer.
   □ c. the Better Business Bureau.

Selection 11: Understanding Ideas

6. The author uses the word "thongs" to mean
   □ a. special climbing shoes.
   □ b. large support posts.
   □ c. thin strips of leather.

7. The author implies that ladders
   □ a. should be purchased carefully.
   □ b. should be painted every year.
   □ c. should be stored in a cool place.

8. The reader can assume that fiberglass
   □ a. is used to make very long ladders.
   □ b. is used to make the steps of ladders.
   □ c. is used in stepladders.

9. The article suggests that
   □ a. fiberglass ladders are very expensive.
   □ b. most people are afraid to climb ladders.
   □ c. wooden ladders last longer than any other type.

10. This article is concerned with
    □ a. the history of ladders.
    □ b. the selection of ladders.
    □ c. the manufacture of ladders.

12. THE FIRST THIRTEEN

Many colonies began in America. Most of the colonists had come from England. It was their mother country. The King of England was their ruler.

Each colony was settled by colonists who came for a purpose. The purpose was not the same in all of the colonies. The colonists in Virginia came to trade. They cut lumber and grew tobacco for sale. The Pilgrims and Puritans, who settled in what is now Massachusetts, came to worship as they pleased. The Quakers came to Pennsylvania and the Roman Catholics came to Maryland for the same purpose.

The Dutch came to trade. They settled in New York. The French colonists settled in Canada and the Spanish colonists settled in Florida. They wanted to trade with the Indians and to teach them the ways of the white man.

One by one the colonies of other nations came under the control of Great Britain. In 1776 there were thirteen British colonies in that part of America that became the United States. These thirteen colonies later became the first thirteen states.

The British people had a king, but they elected representatives who helped make the laws. The lawmaking body was called the Parliament. The people could always tell the lawmakers if they did not like the laws. Sometimes the people were able to have the laws changed.

The king and the Parliament governed the colonies in America. The king let the colonies elect representatives who made some of the local laws. But he sent governors to most of the colonies to carry out the laws of Great Britain. They collected the king's taxes on goods that the colonists brought in from other countries. The colonists were free in many ways. For more than a hundred years they did not say very much against the king and the Parliament.

In 1754 there was a change. A war began between the British colonists and the French. But it was not until 1756 that Great Britain and France actually declared war. In America, the French and the British colonists, each with their Indian allies, helped their mother countries. The war was called the French and Indian War.

The British soldiers and the colonists put up a good fight. Great Britain won the war. A peace treaty was signed in 1763 and Great Britain received Canada. The French colonists in Canada then became subjects of Great Britain.

Selection 12: Recalling Facts

1. The colonists who came to Virginia grew
   - ☐ a. corn.
   - ☐ b. wheat.
   - ☐ c. tobacco.

2. The Quakers settled in the area now known as
   - ☐ a. Ohio.
   - ☐ b. Delaware.
   - ☐ c. Pennsylvania.

3. The Dutch came to America
   - ☐ a. to worship.
   - ☐ b. to trade.
   - ☐ c. to govern themselves.

4. Florida was the site of the first
   - ☐ a. French settlements.
   - ☐ b. Spanish settlements.
   - ☐ c. English settlements.

5. Great Britain and France declared war on each other in the middle
   - ☐ a. 1750s.
   - ☐ b. 1770s.
   - ☐ c. 1790s.

Selection 12: Understanding Ideas

6. During the French and Indian War, colonists
   - ☐ a. sided with their mother countries.
   - ☐ b. supported England.
   - ☐ c. helped the French.

7. As a result of the French and Indian War,
   - ☐ a. the colonists were taxed heavily on foreign goods.
   - ☐ b. many people left France to settle in America.
   - ☐ c. Canada came under English rule.

8. When the settlers first came to America,
   - ☐ a. they set up their own government.
   - ☐ b. they gave up the customs of their homelands.
   - ☐ c. they remained under British rule.

9. Parliament is described as
   - ☐ a. a lawmaking body of people.
   - ☐ b. the first colonial government.
   - ☐ c. an early American court of law.

10. The author implies that the Indians were
    - ☐ a. savage and cruel.
    - ☐ b. strange and timid.
    - ☐ c. friendly and helpful.

13. HIS MASTER'S VOICE

In order to teach a dog to come when he is called, the trainer must use a long rope. One end of the rope should be tied to the dog's collar. Then, he should be allowed to go away on his own. His name should be called along with the word "come." The rope should be jerked at the same time. The command should be repeated several times while the rope is being jerked. The lesson should be repeated until he obeys the command.

When the dog has learned to come when called, the lesson should be taught without the rope. If he does not come when he is called, the rope must be used again. This lesson should be repeated with and without the rope until he learns to come without it.

Another lesson is teaching the dog to walk on the left side of his trainer. A leash is needed for this lesson. The leash is held in the right hand.

The next step in this lesson is to say "heel." If the dog runs forward or lags behind, the lease should be jerked and the command should be repeated. Short, quick jerks are more effective than a continuous pull.

When the dog has learned to walk on the correct side, the lesson should be tried without the leash in an enclosed area. If the dog leaves, the leash should be put back on. The lesson should be repeated with and without the leash.

With the dog at heel position, he can learn how to sit. At the same time, his leash should be pulled back and his hips should be pushed down. This lesson can be repeated with the leash, and later without it, until he will sit on command.

The command "down" means lie down. In the sitting position, the dog is given the command. The leash should then be pulled down. At the same time his shoulders should be pushed gently. If he will not lie down this way, his front legs can be pulled forward until he lies down.

Dogs can be taught to stay in one place. The command "stay" is given while the dog is held in position. The trainer should then back away from him. If he moves, he should be put back in place. The lesson should be repeated until he will stay even when the trainer is out of his sight.

Selection 13: Recalling Facts

1. Training a dog to "heel" requires pulling the leash in
   ☐ a. short, quick jerks.
   ☐ b. long, continuous pulls.
   ☐ c. strong, rapid tugs.

2. The author recommends using
   ☐ a. an enclosed area.   ☐ b. a whip.   ☐ c. a chain.

3. The author discusses teaching a dog to walk
   ☐ a. behind the trainer.   ☐ b. beside the trainer.   ☐ c. in front of the trainer.

4. According to the author, the leash should be fastened to the dog's
   ☐ a. neck.   ☐ b. front paws.   ☐ c. collar.

5. A dog should learn to "stay" even when his trainer
   ☐ a. offers food.   ☐ b. is out of sight.   ☐ c. is in danger.

Selection 13: Understanding Ideas

6. The author implies that the easiest lesson to teach is
   ☐ a. "come."   ☐ b. "sit."   ☐ c. "down."

7. If a dog moves when he is being taught to stay,
   ☐ a. he must be put back in place.
   ☐ b. he must be punished.
   ☐ c. he must be released.

8. In this article the author shows how
   ☐ a. to train a dog.
   ☐ b. to discipline a dog.
   ☐ c. to groom a dog.

9. The command "down" means
   ☐ a. sit down.   ☐ b. roll over.   ☐ c. lie down.

10. If a dog refuses to follow the command "down,"
    ☐ a. he should be rewarded before another attempt is made.
    ☐ b. his front legs should be pulled forward.
    ☐ c. he should not be fed for at least one day.

14. AN UNEXPECTED DRAMA

President Lincoln was leaning slightly forward with his hand on the railing. He had turned his head to look into the audience. Pulling around the flag that decorated the box, he was looking between the pillar and the flag. It was at this moment, 10:15 P.M., that John Wilkes Booth entered the door to box 8 and fired the fatal shot. A single-shot derringer, about six inches long, was fired by Booth at close range. The bullet entered Lincoln's head and lodged close behind the right eye. The President slumped forward in his chair and then backward, never to regain consciousness.

Quickly Major Rathbone sprang upon the assassin. Booth dropped the gun, broke from Rathbone's grasp and lunged at him with a large knife. Rathbone received a deep wound in his left arm above the elbow. Booth placed one hand on the railing to the left of the center pillar and jumped over the railing. Rathbone again seized Booth but caught only his clothing. As he leaped, Booth's right boot struck the framed picture of George Washington. The spur on his right heel caught in the fringe of the flag and brought it down, tearing a strip with it. These obstacles caused the assassin to lose his balance, and he fell awkwardly on the stage. He landed in a kneeling position, with his left leg resting on the stage. In the fall, the large bone of his left leg was fractured about two inches above the ankle.

The actor regained his balance like an athlete and is supposed to have waved his dagger and shouted, "Sic Semper Tyrannis" (Thus always with tyrants), before dashing across the stage. Harry Hawk, seeing Booth coming toward him with a knife, ran through the center doorway on the stage and up a flight of stairs.

Leaving the stage on the north side of the theatre, Booth passed between Laura Keene and young William J. Ferguson, standing near a desk. In the narrow aisle leading from the stage to the rear door, Booth bumped into William Withers, Jr., the orchestra leader. He slashed twice at Withers, cutting his coat and knocking him to the floor before rushing out the door. Grasping the horse's reins from Mr. Burroughs, Booth felled him with the butt end of his knife. He then mounted his horse and rode swiftly from the alley. History had been made.

Selection 14: Recalling Facts

1. Lincoln was shot while he was sitting in
   □ a. the balcony.   □ b. a box seat.   □ c. the front row.

2. Lincoln was shot in
   □ a. the morning.   □ b. the afternoon.   □ c. the evening.

3. The person who first tried to stop Booth was
   □ a. Ferguson.   □ b. Withers.   □ c. Rathbone.

4. Booth injured the greatest number of people with his
   □ a. gun.   □ b. knife.   □ c. cane.

5. In a fall to the stage, Booth fractured his
   □ a. arm.   □ b. ankle.   □ c. leg.

Selection 14: Understanding Ideas

6. The author arranges details
   □ a. in order of importance.
   □ b. in order of time.
   □ c. in order of interest.

7. This article is mostly about
   □ a. Lincoln's attempt to fight off Booth's attack.
   □ b. Booth's escape from the theatre.
   □ c. medical aid given to Lincoln.

8. When Booth shouted, "Sic Semper Tyrannis,"
   □ a. he was referring to himself.
   □ b. he was calling Lincoln a tyrant.
   □ c. he was making a reference to his enemies.

9. The author develops his writing through
   □ a. personal opinions.
   □ b. vivid descriptions.
   □ c. scientific facts.

10. We may conclude that
    □ a. Booth planned his escape carefully in advance.
    □ b. Booth hated all Presidents.
    □ c. Booth was not captured near the theatre.

15. FROM THE ATLANTIC TO THE PACIFIC

America is a very big country. Forty-eight of our fifty states are bounded by the Atlantic Ocean, the Pacific Ocean, Canada, Mexico, and the Gulf of Mexico. Northward on the Pacific Coast is the state of Alaska. And 2,500 miles westward in the Pacific Ocean lie the islands of the state of Hawaii. Together the fifty states of our country contain over three and a half million square miles of land.

Our large country has room for millions of people. They work in many different jobs. They live in cities, in towns, and on farms. They work in the mountains, in the fields, in factories and offices, and on the roads. Many people live near the sea and earn their living from it.

The United States is a great industrial nation. It leads the world in producing automobiles, machinery, chemicals, steel, and textiles. Our chief manufacturing regions are in the Northeast and in the central part of the United States. Big industrial cities are New York, Philadelphia, Boston, Chicago, Detroit, and Pittsburgh. Our country has many other manufacturing centers where many Americans earn their living.

Farming is important work. Farm products are raised almost everywhere in the United States. Where the land is dry, water is brought in to irrigate it. Irrigation, watering the land, helps to make things grow. In southern California, for example, oranges and grapes grow where there once was a great desert.

In the Southern states, cotton and tobacco are grown. In Florida, a Southern state, farmers grow oranges. In the Northwestern states we grow apples. The state of Washington is well known for its apples. Idaho is known for its potatoes. Maine, a Northeastern state, is also known for its potatoes. The richest farming region is in the central part of the United States. This farming area is in the Great Central Plains. This rich farmland grows enough corn and wheat to feed all America, as well as many other countries.

American farmers grow a great deal more food than we need for ourselves. Each year we export hundreds of shiploads of food and crops to other countries.

The Southwestern states are well known for raising cattle. Most of our meat comes from this area. On many large Western ranches and farms, horses and sheep are also raised.

We owe our high standard of living chiefly to our farms and factories.

Selection 15: Recalling Facts

1. The distance between Alaska and Hawaii is about
   - ☐ a. 2,500 miles.
   - ☐ b. 4,000 miles.
   - ☐ c. 5,500 miles.

2. How much land is contained in the 50 states?
   - ☐ a. Over three million square miles
   - ☐ b. Nearly five million square miles
   - ☐ c. More than seven million square miles

3. The United States leads the world in the production of
   - ☐ a. oil.
   - ☐ b. computers.
   - ☐ c. chemicals.

4. A city mentioned is
   - ☐ a. Detroit.
   - ☐ b. Cleveland.
   - ☐ c. Dallas.

5. In southern California farmers grow
   - ☐ a. apples.
   - ☐ b. oranges.
   - ☐ c. peaches.

Selection 15: Understanding Ideas

6. The reader can conclude that
   - ☐ a. potatoes need a cool climate to grow.
   - ☐ b. oranges can survive a light freeze.
   - ☐ c. grapes must be grown in areas of heavy rainfall.

7. This article is concerned mostly with
   - ☐ a. American natural resources.
   - ☐ b. the American labor force.
   - ☐ c. American farm products.

8. The author implies that
   - ☐ a. America grows more wheat than any other country.
   - ☐ b. many countries depend on the United States for food.
   - ☐ c. desert areas are useless for farming.

9. The author mentions Canada as
   - ☐ a. a large cattle-producing country.
   - ☐ b. a friendly country.
   - ☐ c. a neighboring country.

10. We can conclude that, in many areas of the U.S., the soil and climate
    - ☐ a. make abundant crops possible.
    - ☐ b. cause constant problems for the farmer.
    - ☐ c. are improved by scientists.

16. CASTING OUT DEVILS

Savages know little about the nature of disease. Many of them have an idea that sickness is caused by evil spirits which make life miserable for man. They believe these devils hide in sticks and stones, in animals, in earth and sky and jump out to invade and torture the human body. In the South Pacific, certain native tribes still feel sure that sick people are possessed of devils and that unless these spirits are driven out, the person will die. They call these demons Zogos, and they try to frighten them away by mumbling magic words, wearing funny masks and costumes and waving rattles and bones.

Some people in this country believe in Zogos. They believe that you can stave off sicknesses like tuberculosis, measles, or whooping cough by wearing a good-luck charm to scare off the Zogo. Of course, no one has ever really seen a Zogo or held one in his hand. And no one ever will.

We know today that there are many different causes for sickness and death. Many diseases are caused by germs. We sometimes call them microbes because they can be seen only through a special magnifying glass called a microscope.

Some germs or bacteria are useful; others are harmless; but a great many are responsible for much suffering. Different diseases are caused by different bacteria.

Bacteria live everywhere. More of these germs are carried by one person than there are people on the earth. They are alive, take in food, give off wastes, grow, and multiply. What they lack in size they make up for in number. In 24 hours a single germ will produce 281,000,000,000,000 other germs, each one capable of doing the same.

Fortunately, a great many bacteria die off by themselves, and a great many do no harm. Otherwise we would be sick all the time. We should be concerned about those that do cause sickness.

Most disease germs grow best at body temperature. High temperatures usually kill them. Freezing does not hurt them, though it does keep them from multiplying. They are not lovers of the light. They like to breed in the dark. Direct sunlight kills them. Most bacteria need air but some grow only in absence of air. Others can get along with or without it. They need moisture to grow. Their favorite homes are milk, eggs, meats, shellfish, poultry and water.

Selection 16: Recalling Facts

1. According to the author, a Zogo is
   □ a. a good spirit. □ b. a demon. □ c. a witch doctor.

2. Germs are sometimes called
   □ a. microbes. □ b. genes. □ c. cells.

3. Freezing temperatures
   □ a. kill germs.
   □ b. keep germs from multiplying.
   □ c. help germs multiply.

4. Most bacteria cannot survive in
   □ a. light. □ b. air. □ c. moisture.

5. Germs breed rapidly in
   □ a. bread. □ b. fruit. □ c. eggs.

Selection 16: Understanding Ideas

6. The author states that
   □ a. all germs are harmful.
   □ b. some germs can live in a vacuum.
   □ c. large germs can be seen with the naked eye.

7. The body is a favorite breeding place for germs because
   □ a. it is warm.
   □ b. it is always in motion.
   □ c. it is exposed to sunlight.

8. Primitive tribes think of germs as
   □ a. gods who are angry with them.
   □ b. living things that can be frightened away.
   □ c. invisible cells.

9. This article is concerned mostly with
   □ a. illnesses of primitive peoples.
   □ b. modern medicine.
   □ c. bacteria.

10. We can conclude that
    □ a. germs multiply rapidly.
    □ b. germs are difficult to kill.
    □ c. germs do not live in outer space.

17. FELINE FRIENDS

Domestic cats are classified as either long haired or short haired. Long-haired types were developed in Persia and Afghanistan. Short-haired types were developed in Egypt, Europe, and Asia.

Usually, short-haired cats are active and playful, and easier to care for than long-haired ones. Long-haired cats are quiet, stay-at-home pets, but they sometimes need extra care because of their long hair.

A person can buy a bed for his cat or he can make one from a box or basket. The bed should be in a quiet part of the home away from drafts. It should be lined with a blanket, cushion, or discarded clothing. The bedding must be kept clean.

A cat should have a balanced diet. Cat foods from the market usually provide good nourishment under normal conditions.

A cat should not be given small bones that are likely to splinter, especially bones from pork or poultry.

Although a cat may lick his bowl clean, it should be washed after each use. Fresh water should be available at all times. The same bowl should not be used for water as is used for food.

Kittens usually are weaned when they are about six to eight weeks old. They keep some of their baby teeth until they reach six months. They must be fed four times a day until they lose their baby teeth.

As the kittens grow, they will gradually eat more food. The number of feedings will decrease to twice daily by the time they are eight or nine months old.

Normally cats should not be bathed. They clean their fur by licking it. If a cat gets dirty, he may be bathed in warm, soapy water.

His skin must be rubbed thoroughly with a cloth. The water must be kept out of his eyes and ears. He must be rinsed in warm water and dried thoroughly. He must be kept indoors until completely dry.

Cleaning preparations for cats also may be used.

A cat must be brushed often, especially if he has long hair. Brushing gets loose hairs out of his coat that otherwise would get on the furniture and rugs.

Knots form in the coats of long-haired cats. The knots can be pulled apart with a comb. If that fails, blunt scissors can be used.

Selection 17: Recalling Facts

1. Long-haired cats were developed in
   □ a. Egypt.   □ b. Asia.   □ c. Persia.

2. Long-haired cats tend to be
   □ a. quiet.   □ b. active.   □ c. playful.

3. A cat should not be given
   □ a. chicken bones.   □ b. beef bones.   □ c. lamb bones.

4. Until kittens lose their baby teeth, they must be fed
   □ a. twice a day.   □ b. three times a day.   □ c. four times a day.

5. Kittens are usually weaned when they are no older than
   □ a. four weeks.   □ b. eight weeks.   □ c. twelve weeks.

Selection 17: Understanding Ideas

6. The author implies that kittens must be fed often because
   □ a. they like to eat.
   □ b. they have small stomachs.
   □ c. they digest food slowly.

7. The author recommends
   □ a. bathing cats at least once a month.
   □ b. using scissors for knots in fur.
   □ c. giving cats vitamins.

8. From the facts provided, the reader can assume that
   □ a. water is harmful to a cat's ears.
   □ b. cats enjoy sleeping in paper bags.
   □ c. domestic cats are related to tigers and lions.

9. Cat food that can be purchased in the market
   □ a. is often lacking in important vitamins.
   □ b. contains adequate nutrition for most cats.
   □ c. should not be offered at every meal.

10. We can conclude from the article that
    □ a. cats are fussy eaters.
    □ b. cats are easy to train.
    □ c. cats require a minimum of care.

18. THE LAND OF BAGPIPES

Scotland is the northern part of Great Britain. The Scots are a proud people. They are especially proud of their fighting skills. They claim theirs is the only country in Europe which has never been conquered.

As one travels north, he finds the climate turning colder. That is, colder for visitors, but "just brisk" to the Scots.

Some of the world's finest tweeds come from the cities and towns around the River Tweed in the section of Scotland closest to England. And since almost every part of the country touches the sea, some of the best fish dishes are served in restaurants and hotels.

Most visitors to Scotland start with the capital city of Edinburgh. Almost as soon as they arrive, they know that this is Robert Burns' country since his monument can be seen in the center of the city.

Only a short journey away is Linlithgow Castle where Mary Stuart, Queen of Scots, was born in 1542. Edinburgh Castle is another sight sure to be pointed out to visitors.

On a clear day one has a good view of the city from the castle. Jewels and crowns of ancient Scottish rulers are displayed inside.

Only a short journey away is the city of Glasgow on the Clyde River. While many visitors explore this modern city, most head on steamers for the island resorts which are found in the area.

Scotland is the home of golf and there are excellent courses at St. Andrews. While this ancient town is best known to foreign visitors for its courses, it is also the site of St. Andrews University, the oldest institution of higher learning in Scotland. Famed for its ghosts, Glamis Castle can be visited on the way to see Balmoral Castle, the Highland residence of the Royal Family. The sound of bagpipes can be heard when the Queen is in residence.

As one goes further north, Scotland becomes more mountainous. Flocks of sheep can be seen on the hillsides and the Loch Ness monster also is seen once in a while. Many claim to have seen the monster after making one or more stops to sample the whisky for which Scotland is known.

Loch Lomond has no monster to attract visitors but it is located in one of the prettiest areas of Scotland. Each year it draws thousands of hikers. Hiking is a popular way to see the countryside.

Selection 18: Recalling Facts

1. Scotland is located in
   □ a. northern Great Britain.
   □ b. western Great Britain.
   □ c. eastern Great Britain.

2. The author mentions that the Scots are
   □ a. skillful.　　□ b. proud.　　□ c. clever.

3. Scotland is famous for its
   □ a. tweeds.　　□ b. flowers.　　□ c. cheeses.

4. People travel to St. Andrews to play
   □ a. tennis.　　□ b. cricket.　　□ c. golf.

5. Scotland raises many
   □ a. sheep.　　□ b. cows.　　□ c. pigs.

Selection 18: Understanding Ideas

6. The article suggests that Scotland shares a border with
   □ a. Ireland.　　□ b. Wales.　　□ c. England.

7. The Scots claim that
   □ a. England does not give them enough freedom in government.
   □ b. Ireland is unfriendly toward them.
   □ c. Scotland has never been conquered in war.

8. The reader can infer that
   □ a. Scotland has many beaches.
   □ b. England is very cold during the summer months.
   □ c. Wales is west of England.

9. Bagpipes are played in Scotland
   □ a. when a famous artist dies.
   □ b. when the queen visits the area.
   □ c. when a storm is expected.

10. The author feels that the Loch Ness monster
    □ a. is a danger to local residents.
    □ b. should be captured.
    □ c. does not really exist.

When the material is found, lay your fire by piling your tinder in a close pile about the size of a hat. Then crisscross the smallest and driest kindling over the tinder. With your back to the wind, light the tinder. The wind will quickly spread the flames through the pile. If there is no wind, fan the fire with something. Add the rest of the kindling. When the fire is roaring, add fuelwood to it as needed.

If the fire is used for cooking, there are a number of styles that can be copied from the woodsman. The trapper's fire uses two fairly large logs laid on each side of the fire. It helps to flatten the top of the logs with an ax. Then pots and pans can rest on the logs, and it is a long, narrow, controlled fire that is easy to fuel and easy to cook on.

Some like the lazyman or star fire, where longer logs come into the fire like spokes from a wheel. The logs are pushed in as they burn and need a larger clearing for safety.

The picturesque hunter's fire has forked sticks supporting a cross pole over the fire from which pothooks can hold the pots and pans at any desired height.

There are many other choices including pit or trench fires to save fuel, rock fireplaces, platform fireplaces, or the reflector fires that are built in front of a tent.

Flames are best for boiling food, but coals are best for broiling. To get flames, add a pine knot, split kindling or dry twigs. To get coals, you must wait for the wood to burn down to coals, or you might add charred brands or charcoal from an old fire if available. Allow a full hour from the time the fire is started until the cooking is started.

If the fire is to last a long time in a campfire or in the home fireplace, pack round logs rather tightly over the fire and cover them partly with ashes from the fire.

Don't burn the house down or mar a vacation with carelessness. Fire is a wonderful ally but a dangerous enemy. When camping, clear a ten-foot circle down to mineral soil or rock. In the home fireplace, there should be a good, strong fire screen to prevent sparks or brands from popping or rolling into the room.

Selection 19: Recalling Facts

1. The fire which looks like a wheel with spokes is called
   □ a. the lazyman fire.   □ b. the hunter's fire.   □ c. the trench fire.

2. What is the best fire condition for boiling food?
   □ a. Flames   □ b. Coals   □ c. Smoke

3. According to this selection, adding pine knots to a fire creates
   □ a. a fragrance.   □ b. coals.   □ c. flames.

4. How much time does a fire need to become suitable for broiling?
   □ a. 15 minutes   □ b. 30 minutes   □ c. 60 minutes

5. A fire which supposedly saves fuel is the
   □ a. star fire.   □ b. hunter's fire.   □ c. pit fire.

Selection 19: Understanding Ideas

6. The "trapper's fire" is used
   □ a. to cook food.
   □ b. to keep warm after dark.
   □ c. to lure animals out of the woods.

7. The article suggests that the largest size of wood is called
   □ a. tinder.   □ b. fuelwood.   □ c. kindling.

8. Using ashes to partially cover logs on a fire
   □ a. puts out the fire.
   □ b. makes the heat more intense.
   □ c. makes the fire last longer.

9. In this article the author warns against
   □ a. carelessness in handling fire.
   □ b. using green wood to start a fire.
   □ c. lighting campfires without permission.

10. The reader may conclude that building a fire is
    □ a. mostly luck.
    □ b. a skill that most people cannot learn.
    □ c. an art which requires planning.

20. JOB HUNTING

Soon after an immigrant arrives in the United States, he probably looks for a job. Sometimes friends or relatives find work for him before he arrives. If not, there are many things he can do to get work.

The newcomer may be able to get work through the United States Employment Service. It has offices all over the country. In big cities the United States Employment Service (USES) has offices where he can apply for different types of jobs. These offices have jobs for professional workers, clerical workers, domestic workers, and for people who work in trades. A professional worker is one who does a job that requires special education. Clerical workers are office workers. A typist is a clerical worker. So are stenographers, bookkeepers, file clerks, and secretaries. A domestic worker is someone who works at household jobs, such as a housemaid, a chambermaid, a family cook, or an office cleaner. Carpenters and bricklayers work in trades.

There are also private employment agencies in many cities. They, too, help people find jobs. When a worker gets a job through a private agency, he is charged a fee for its work. The newcomer may find work by applying for a job at one or more of these agencies.

In the classified ads section of the newspaper, there are advertisements about job openings. Jobs are listed under the heading "Help Wanted." Both men and women can apply for these jobs.

Many ads ask for a letter from the person looking for a job. The letter should include information regarding age, education, experience, and references.

Most jobs require references, the names and addresses of former employers, or a letter from them. If he has not worked in the United States, the newcomer may give the names and addresses of former employers in the old country. He may impress the person who is interviewing him with his experience and ability and be hired without references.

Most trades in the United States are unionized. In a union shop, all workers must join the union. In a nonunion shop, workers may or may not belong to a union. Unions try to find jobs for their unemployed members.

A job is only a beginning. As the newcomer learns more English, more about the United States, and more about the educational opportunities in the United States, he may want to look for better jobs.

Selection 20: Recalling Facts

1. In a union shop, all workers must
   - ☐ a. have Blue Cross coverage.
   - ☐ b. join the union.
   - ☐ c. work overtime.

2. Carpenters and bricklayers are considered
   - ☐ a. administrators.   ☐ b. tradesmen.   ☐ c. domestic employees.

3. When a worker gets a job through a private agency, he is
   - ☐ a. charged a fee.   ☐ b. paid little.   ☐ c. accepted on trial.

4. When applying for a job by letter, you should include your
   - ☐ a. hobbies.   ☐ b. height.   ☐ c. education.

5. The name and address of a former employer is called
   - ☐ a. a reference.   ☐ b. an application.   ☐ c. a union letter.

Selection 20: Understanding Ideas

6. A newcomer who applies for work with two or more agencies
   - ☐ a. is breaking the law.
   - ☐ b. is increasing his chances for work.
   - ☐ c. is ignoring an old custom.

7. People who come to this country to work
   - ☐ a. often have relatives who have found work for them.
   - ☐ b. usually bring their birth certificates with them.
   - ☐ c. sometimes go on welfare rolls immediately.

8. A domestic worker might be expected
   - ☐ a. to drive the family car.
   - ☐ b. to operate heavy machinery.
   - ☐ c. to take dictation.

9. The author implies that
   - ☐ a. many newcomers find better jobs after they learn English.
   - ☐ b. most employment agencies have offices in foreign countries.
   - ☐ c. some unions make newcomers pay higher dues than native workers.

10. We can conclude that
    - ☐ a. American workers are the best paid in the world.
    - ☐ b. work is available for the newcomer who applies for it.
    - ☐ c. unions are against the hiring of foreign workers.

21. CROWNS AND THRONES

Life was sometimes stormy for the men who sat on the British throne. One ruler, Charles, was executed in 1647 after a civil war broke out when he tried to reduce the power of Parliament. For 11 years the land was run as a protectorate by military men. With the death of the leader, Oliver Cromwell, in 1658, the revolt lost its followers. The people put a Stuart king back on the throne in 1660. But the revolt had established for all time the power of the Parliament and the role of the ruler.

Kings and queens of the House of Hanover ruled Britain from 1714 until 1901. This was the era of the great growth of industry in Great Britain. Along with it came the growth of the British Empire as Britons searched for raw materials and markets. It was also a time of wars.

Defeat forced France to turn over its colonies in Canada to Britain in 1763. A few years later, Britain lost its North American colonies, except those in Canada, when they revolted, fought for their freedom and finally declared their independence in 1776.

The Industrial Revolution in Britain poured goods and machines into the markets of the world. From the far reaches of the Empire came the raw materials. A vast fleet of British ships carried the raw materials to Britain. The finished products were taken around the world.

Along with the products, Britain was giving the world a more valuable item, industrial know-how. Other nations copied British products and methods. Soon these nations were manufacturing their own products and competing with Britain for the world's markets.

Queen Victoria, a ruler who gave her name to an age of refinement and progress, guided the destiny of the British people from 1837 until 1901. In the last year of her reign, the millions of men who worked in factories gained a voice in the political life of the country through the Labor Representation Committee. This group was to be renamed the Labor Party in 1906.

The Victorian and Edwardian eras came to an abrupt end with the many disasters of World War I. The four years of war cost Britain almost an entire generation of her youth, and her economic position slipped considerably.

King George V came to the throne in 1910. In 1917, faced with rising anti-German feelings, he proclaimed that the royal house would thereafter be named Windsor.

Selection 21: Recalling Facts

1. Which ruler was executed in the middle 1600s after a civil war?
    ☐ a. Charles ☐ b. Henry ☐ c. Richard

2. During the 1700s and 1800s, kings and queens were from the House of
    ☐ a. Hanover. ☐ b. Stewart. ☐ c. Tudor.

3. The French colonies in Canada were turned over to Britain in
    ☐ a. the middle 1600s. ☐ b. the middle 1700s. ☐ c. the middle 1800s.

4. Many countries of the world copied England's
    ☐ a. naval system.
    ☐ b. manufacturing methods.
    ☐ c. political system.

5. Under the rule of Queen Victoria, England
    ☐ a. progressed. ☐ b. declined. ☐ c. struggled.

Selection 21: Understanding Ideas

6. The article suggests that English kings and queens rule
    ☐ a. for indefinite periods of time.
    ☐ b. until they are replaced.
    ☐ c. for a specific number of years.

7. The author implies that
    ☐ a. Queen Victoria was a harsh ruler.
    ☐ b. England has few raw materials of her own.
    ☐ c. Canada was given back to France after World War I.

8. A protectorate is a government controlled by
    ☐ a. one powerful ruler.
    ☐ b. a group of people.
    ☐ c. a foreign power.

9. Over the years England has been most admired for her
    ☐ a. military power.
    ☐ b. industrial know-how.
    ☐ c. aid to less fortunate countries.

10. This article is concerned primarily with
    ☐ a. cruel kings and queens.
    ☐ b. world trade agreements.
    ☐ c. England's position in the world.

22. GOING TO THE DOGS

The breeds of dogs are divided into six groups. These groups are sporting dogs, hounds, terriers, working dogs, toy dogs, and non-sporting dogs.

In each of these groups the dogs are bred for a special purpose. Many dogs serve the purpose for which they were bred. But many others have become favorite household pets. Some dogs have cropped ears and tails for purposes of style or to meet dog show requirements.

Any of the breeds of dogs can be kept as pets. Breeding, size, and other features, however, make some more suitable than others.

If one buys a purebred dog, he can select one that has traits best suited to his needs. He must be sure to get the certificate that gives the date of birth and the registration number.

It is not necessary to buy a purebred dog to have a good pet. Many mixed breeds make excellent pets. Often one can get a mixed-breed dog free or for a small fee from a dog pound, animal shelter, or pet shop. A dog should be examined by a veterinarian as soon as possible after he is taken home.

A dog should be trained to relieve himself outdoors on his owner's property so he will not annoy neighbors. In an apartment, a dog owner may need to teach his pet to use newspapers first and then to go outdoors after he has learned to control himself.

When a dog shows signs of restlessness, such as turning and sniffing, he should be taken outside. He must be left outside long enough for him to relieve himself. Then he can be brought in immediately. When the weather is bad, he may not want to go outside. But if he is taken out anyway, he will finish quickly and come back inside.

When he has an accident, he must be scolded. Then he should be taken to his spot outdoors. The floor must be scrubbed enough to remove even the slightest odor because dogs return to the same place if they smell the odor.

The dog should be allowed to go outside at night, early in the morning, and after he has eaten or played. He will have accidents, but in a week or two, he should know what he is expected to do.

If an owner must housebreak his dog on newspapers, he should spread several layers in a little used part of the apartment. After the dog has learned to use newspapers, they should be taken away except at night. In the daytime he can be taken outdoors when he must go. As he grows older, he will learn to control himself. Then the newspapers can be removed.

Selection 22: Recalling Facts

1. Dogs with cropped ears are seen most often
   □ a. in dog shows. □ b. in hunting areas. □ c. in sled races.

2. Most purebred dogs are sold with
   □ a. birth certificates. □ b. a written guarantee. □ c. a license.

3. When a dog has an accident, he should be
   □ a. ignored. □ b. scolded. □ c. slapped.

4. A dog is usually trained after he has been taught for
   □ a. three days. □ b. two weeks. □ c. one month.

5. The author suggests housebreaking a dog by using
   □ a. a litter box. □ b. an old blanket. □ c. newspapers.

Selection 22: Understanding Ideas

6. This article is mostly about
   □ a. teaching a dog tricks.
   □ b. buying and training a young dog.
   □ c. taking care of a dog that is ill.

7. A veterinarian is
   □ a. an animal doctor.
   □ b. a person who trains animals.
   □ c. a person who owns many dogs.

8. When a dog begins turning and sniffing,
   □ a. he is suffering from a high fever.
   □ b. he is showing that he is hungry.
   □ c. he is indicating that he wants to go out.

9. The author implies that
   □ a. a mixed-breed dog does not usually live as long as a purebred.
   □ b. dogs often eat too much food.
   □ c. a hound is not considered to be a sporting dog.

10. The reader can infer that
    □ a. most purebred dogs cost more than $100.
    □ b. mixed-breed dogs are less expensive than purebreds.
    □ c. purebreds are more popular than mixed breeds.

23. JOHN FITZGERALD KENNEDY

The Kennedy half dollar was first made in 1964 as an honor to the late President.

John Fitzgerald Kennedy, 35th President of the United States, is remembered as an active and eager President. He entered the White House in 1961 at the age of 43, one of our youngest presidents. Even by then, he had lived a full and colorful life. After graduation from Harvard College, he toured Europe and visited Great Britain. In the same year, he published his first book, *Why England Slept,* a study of pre-World War II British politics.

As a junior navy lieutenant during World War II, he commanded a PT boat in the Pacific. His boat was hit by a Japanese destroyer. The collision dumped the crew of twelve men into the ocean in the middle of flaming gasoline. Kennedy swam to a nearby island with the rest of his crew. He towed a wounded crewman by a life jacket which he gripped in his teeth. This swim took five hours. It won him the Navy and Marine Corps Medal for courage and bravery.

Kennedy's youth and spirit captured the hearts of the American people. His speeches were not only words, but calls to duty and action. He led the nation to a new belief in the freedoms of America. He called upon people to meet the demands of a new age for our country and for the whole free world.

Kennedy's dream for America went into the homes and shops of cities around the world. People began to look to America with new hopes. His life was cut short by a sniper's bullet on November 23, 1963, as he rode in a motorcade through downtown Dallas, Texas. He had been President for less than three years. The nation was plunged into grief as he was laid to rest in Arlington National Cemetery.

The back of the Kennedy half dollar bears the Presidential Coat of Arms. It features the American spread eagle holding the olive branch of peace in one claw and a bundle of arrows meaning defense in the other. The Presidential Seal was first used about 1878. It was probably taken from the Great Seal of the United States. According to custom, the eagle faces to the left toward the bundle of arrows during wartime. It faces to the right toward honor and the olive branches in peacetime.

Selection 23: Recalling Facts

1. The Kennedy half dollar was first issued in
   - ☐ a. 1964.
   - ☐ b. 1966.
   - ☐ c. 1968.

2. Kennedy became President at the age of
   - ☐ a. 38.
   - ☐ b. 43.
   - ☐ c. 47.

3. At one time, Kennedy commanded a PT boat in
   - ☐ a. the Atlantic.
   - ☐ b. the Pacific.
   - ☐ c. the Mediterranean.

4. Kennedy was President for less than
   - ☐ a. one year.
   - ☐ b. two years.
   - ☐ c. three years.

5. After graduation from college, Kennedy visited
   - ☐ a. Great Britain.
   - ☐ b. Mexico.
   - ☐ c. Russia.

Selection 23: Understanding Ideas

6. The author offers proof that Kennedy was
   - ☐ a. heroic.
   - ☐ b. sincere.
   - ☐ c. hardworking.

7. According to the author, Kennedy's speeches
   - ☐ a. helped to improve relations between America and Russia.
   - ☐ b. aroused interest in the space program.
   - ☐ c. gave Americans new hope for America.

8. The author concludes the article with a discussion of
   - ☐ a. Kennedy's naval career.
   - ☐ b. Kennedy's death and funeral.
   - ☐ c. the Kennedy half dollar.

9. Before he became President, Kennedy
   - ☐ a. wrote a book about England.
   - ☐ b. was the American ambassador to England.
   - ☐ c. lived in England for several years.

10. Kennedy thought that the world was
    - ☐ a. entering a new age.
    - ☐ b. heading towards nuclear war.
    - ☐ c. falling into the grips of inflation.

24. LOST IN THE WOODS

If you get lost in the woods, a little knowledge can turn what some people call a hardship into an enjoyable stay away from the woes of modern society. Many a high-pressured businessman would willingly get himself lost in the outdoors for several days if he only knew how enjoyable it can be with a minimum of know-how.

When you think you are lost, sit down on a log or a rock or lean against a tree and recite something that you have memorized to bring your mind to a point where it is under control.

Don't run wildly helter-skelter! If you must move, don't follow streams unless you know the stream, and in that case you are not lost. Streams normally flow through swampland before they reach a lake or a river. Though there are more edible plants per square inch in a swamp, there may also be quicksand, poisonous snakes, and other hazards.

If you must walk, walk uphill. At the top of most hills and mountains are trails leading back to civilization. If there are no trails, you are much easier to find above the timberline or on top of a hill, and you may even spot a highway or a railroad from this vantage point.

Nowadays, the first way someone will look for you is by air. In a swamp or in dense growth you are very hard to spot.

Any time that you go into the woods, somebody should know where you are going and when you expect to return. Also, when someone comes looking, you should be able to signal to them.

The best way that you can signal in the daytime is with a good smoky fire. In most of our country either a fire tower or airplane will quickly spot the smoke. A fire warden will come to your rescue. At night, a bright fire will bring help if someone knows you are lost.

In the old days whenever you got lost, you could fire your weapon three times. Today lots of hunters fire a half dozen shots without hitting game. However, if you save your shots until after dark and fire one shot, then wait for a half hour or so and fire another, in less time than it takes to get your third shot off a game warden or the ranger should be there to show you the way out of the woods.

Selection 24: Recalling Facts

1. If a person becomes lost and wants to walk, he should move
    ☐ a. uphill.   ☐ b. downhill.   ☐ c. northerly.

2. Nowadays, the first way someone will look for you is by
    ☐ a. vehicle.   ☐ b. foot.   ☐ c. plane.

3. The best way to signal for help, night or day, is with
    ☐ a. a mirror.   ☐ b. broken branches.   ☐ c. a fire.

4. Years ago a signal for help meant firing a weapon how many times?
    ☐ a. Two   ☐ b. Three   ☐ c. Four

5. The kinds of plants found in swamps are usually
    ☐ a. deceptive.   ☐ b. edible.   ☐ c. poisonous.

Selection 24: Understanding Ideas

6. In swamps and dense growth, a person is
    ☐ a. hard to find.
    ☐ b. much safer.
    ☐ c. quite visible.

7. If you become lost, the first action the author advises is
    ☐ a. searching immediately for help.
    ☐ b. retracing your steps into the woods.
    ☐ c. sitting down and reciting a poem.

8. Following a stream may
    ☐ a. allow you to find your way out.
    ☐ b. take you deeper into unknown territory.
    ☐ c. expose you to unexpected dangers.

9. The author implies that becoming lost should not be
    ☐ a. pleasurable.
    ☐ b. frightening.
    ☐ c. enlightening.

10. The author of this selection wishes to be
    ☐ a. instructive.
    ☐ b. controversial.
    ☐ c. scientific.

25. GOVERNMENT BY THE PEOPLE

Our democracy is known as a republican form of government. The people choose the President and other people to act for them. Democratic government began in America's earliest days and continues today.

In 1620 the Pilgrims agreed to govern themselves. While they were still on their little ship, the *Mayflower,* they wrote the Mayflower Compact. They set up their own government. In this Compact they agreed that together they would frame just and equal laws.

In 1776, the colonists decided that they could not continue to live under British rule. They decided to separate from Great Britain and form their own government.

Their leaders signed the Declaration of Independence which said, ". . . governments are instituted among men, deriving their just powers from the consent of the governed . . . ." This means that in our country the people rule themselves. The government is the servant, not the master of the people.

After the colonists were free from Great Britain, they had to form a new government. For months their leaders talked about different plans of government. The Continental Congress chose a group to make a plan. They drew up a plan for a central government. It was called the Articles of Confederation. By 1781 it was accepted by all thirteen states.

The United States formed a Congress under the Articles. The Congress made the laws. It carried on the business of the government. But there was no President. And there were no courts to protect the rights of the people. The Congress did not have much power to carry on its work. The new union of states had no money. This form of government under the Articles was not a success. The plan had not worked well.

The young United States had to create a form of government strong enough to protect itself against foreign enemies and strong enough to solve its own problems. The Congress asked the states to send men to a convention to change the Articles of Confederation.

This meeting, to plan for a new government, was called the Constitutional Convention. It met on May 25, 1787. The delegates elected George Washington as their chairman. All but one state, Rhode Island, sent delegates to this convention. Among the men who helped to write the Constitution of the United States were such famous men as Benjamin Franklin, James Madison, and Alexander Hamilton. The delegates decided that they could not change the Articles of Confederation. They needed a new plan of government. They began to write one.

Selection 25: Recalling Facts

1. The colonies decided to form their own government in
    - ☐ a. 1725.
    - ☐ b. 1776.
    - ☐ c. 1793.

2. In a democracy the government is the
    - ☐ a. master of the people.
    - ☐ b. servant of the people.
    - ☐ c. slave of the people.

3. The Articles of Confederation was accepted by
    - ☐ a. 9 states.
    - ☐ b. 11 states.
    - ☐ c. 13 states.

4. Under the Articles of Confederation, the U.S. could have
    - ☐ a. a President.
    - ☐ b. a Congress.
    - ☐ c. a court system.

5. What state did not send delegates to the Constitutional Convention?
    - ☐ a. Connecticut
    - ☐ b. Georgia
    - ☐ c. Rhode Island

Selection 25: Understanding Ideas

6. According to the author, the Articles of Confederation
    - ☐ a. was a failure.
    - ☐ b. was revised by the Constitutional Convention.
    - ☐ c. was successful for many years.

7. The article states that the Articles of Confederation
    - ☐ a. did not protect a citizen's rights.
    - ☐ b. did not allow the President to travel abroad.
    - ☐ c. did not allow the use of British money.

8. The Pilgrims are mentioned as an example of
    - ☐ a. a group which came to America seeking religious freedom.
    - ☐ b. a band of poor and homeless travelers.
    - ☐ c. a group which believed in democratic government.

9. The author implies that the plan for the Continental Congress
    - ☐ a. was drawn up without much thought.
    - ☐ b. was adopted from the English system of government.
    - ☐ c. was the result of many discussions about government.

10. We can conclude that the U.S. Government is strong enough
    - ☐ a. to solve most of its internal problems.
    - ☐ b. to conquer any country in the world.
    - ☐ c. to prevent wars within the country.

26. PREPARING FOR A FLOOD

During floods there is a fire hazard. Electric power should be shut off. Gas jets or valves should be closed. And open flames should be doused. If you need power, locate powerlines above flood levels.

Power to electric appliances should be turned off before they are flooded. After flooding, the appliances should be cleaned and dried before being used again. Rugs and furniture should be cleaned after flooding.

Erosion of lawns and of fields can be decreased through proper placement of trees and shrubbery.

Fences and hedges can be arranged to reduce the effects of rushing floodwaters. Your county engineer, agricultural agent, or city engineer can advise you. Natural dunes along coastal areas should be kept because they provide fine protection against tidal action.

Roadbeds can be given greater protection by reducing the scouring action of floodwaters. Culverts and other openings should be large enough to handle most floods without overflowing and washing away the highway fill. Trees or shrubs can be planted on the slopes of road fills to resist washing.

If you live in a flood plain or if you have equipment in the areas subject to flooding, you should have a plan to remove valuables in times of emergency. Some goods and equipment can be lifted to higher levels in the same structure. You should be prepared to build platforms or to strengthen supports of available shelves.

You should know which roads flood at various flood heights to assure your safe escape from areas that are expected to be flooded to great depths.

Grain should be stored at levels above the floods or in structures that are flood proofed. Storage of large amounts should be at elevations above flooding.

Where the depths of flooding are not expected to be great, homes and other structures can be raised. They can be jacked up and their foundation walls raised at reasonable cost. Sometimes buildings can be moved to sites which are above the expected flood heights.

If you are building a new home, locate it free from flooding or design it to withstand any flooding with minimum losses.

In rural areas, there should be openings in the structures and in the surrounding fences or walls which will permit access to higher land for the livestock and for removing equipment.

The best time, and most economical way, to flood proof is when you build your home or other structures.

Selection 26: Recalling Facts

1. This article states that during floods there is a danger of
   ☐ a. disease.   ☐ b. fire.   ☐ c. looting.

2. After a flood, electrical appliances should be
   ☐ a. cleaned.   ☐ b. repaired.   ☐ c. thrown away.

3. Trees and shrubs help to
   ☐ a. prevent flooding.   ☐ b. protect buildings.   ☐ c. decrease erosion.

4. County engineers
   ☐ a. predict floods.   ☐ b. give advice.   ☐ c. build bridges.

5. The scouring action of floodwaters can be prevented
   ☐ a. on roadbeds.   ☐ b. near hedges.   ☐ c. around livestock.

Selection 26: Understanding Ideas

6. When the author suggests raising a building, he means that
   ☐ a. a second story should be added.
   ☐ b. the foundation should be made higher.
   ☐ c. it should be built on high pilings.

7. The author of this selection
   ☐ a. gives advice on flood safety.
   ☐ b. describes how to flood-proof a new house.
   ☐ c. suggests different ways of leaving a flooded area.

8. When flooding begins
   ☐ a. shrubs should be transplanted.
   ☐ b. windows should be boarded.
   ☐ c. power should be turned off.

9. This article does not discuss
   ☐ a. the causes of floods.
   ☐ b. the storage of grain in flood areas.
   ☐ c. the removal of valuables during floods.

10. We can conclude that
    ☐ a. man is now able to stop floods.
    ☐ b. flooding occurs along ocean property.
    ☐ c. rarely steps can be taken to reduce flood damage.

27. AN EFFECTIVE DIET

If you intend to start a reducing program, it is wise to check first with your doctor. He can tell if you are in good physical shape for reducing. If you are, he can tell you how much weight to lose and the number of calories to have in your daily diet. He can tell you if exercise or other physical activity is needed.

Plan meals around familiar foods. The only effective diet is the one that is followed daily. For this reason, it is wise to plan meals around foods which are satisfying and are part of the family's way of eating.

When you have reached the right weight, simple additions can be made to the diet so that you can keep your weight.

It is important to create patterns of eating which can be followed when proper weight is attained. Strange and unusual foods and food combinations may seem like a great solution to the dieter's problem, but they are nearly always poor choices as regular food. As a result, the dieter soon may become unhappy and go back to the old food habits that caused the weight gain.

When you plan meals, follow a reliable food plan to be sure of getting the nutritionally important kinds of food. Many reducing diets which include only a few foods are low in needed vitamins and minerals. Such diets should not be followed for any length of time.

Choose low-calorie foods. Avoid such items as added fats, gravies, sauces, fried foods, fatty meats, sweets, pastries, cookies, cakes, alcoholic and soft drinks, and cream.

Season foods with spices, herbs, vinegars, or tart fruit juices to give variety and add interest.

Learn to like cereal or fruit with little or no added sugar. Choose coffee and tea with little or no sugar and cream.

Budget your calories to take care of special occasions, such as holiday meals and parties. Save on calories from other meals to allow extra calories for these.

Snacks, too, can be part of your diet if you plan for them. For example, a piece of fruit or a crisp vegetable, milk, or a simple dessert saved from mealtime can be eaten between meals.

Keep busy so you will not be tempted to eat foods which are not included in your planned meals.

Take advantage of daily chances to increase activities. For instance, walk, rather than ride, whenever possible.

Selection 27: Recalling Facts

1. Before starting a diet, a person should
   □ a. weigh himself.   □ b. increase exercise.   □ c. see a doctor.

2. Meals should be planned around foods which are
   □ a. familiar.   □ b. exotic.   □ c. tasty.

3. The author advises a person on a diet to avoid
   □ a. alcohol.   □ b. lean meat.   □ c. seafood.

4. For the person on a diet, spices, herbs, and vinegars
   □ a. add weight.   □ b. cause indigestion.   □ c. give variety.

5. The only effective diet is the one which is
   □ a. totally salt-free.   □ b. faithfully followed.   □ c. immediately effective.

Selection 27: Understanding Ideas

6. The author suggests that a person on a diet should
   □ a. eat basically what other members of the family eat.
   □ b. restrict intake of large quantities of water.
   □ c. develop a liking for high protein foods.

7. The author warns that many diets
   □ a. are too expensive for most people to follow.
   □ b. ignore essential nutrition.
   □ c. appeal to the person who does not need to lose weight.

8. The author implies that most people gain weight because of
   □ a. inadequate exercise.
   □ b. poor eating habits.
   □ c. indifference to one's own appearance.

9. Dieting, as recommended in this article, allows
   □ a. birthday parties and holiday meals.
   □ b. eating candy between meals.
   □ c. large helpings at each meal.

10. This article leads the reader to believe that
   □ a. calorie requirements are different for each person.
   □ b. most doctors do not approve of dieting.
   □ c. losing weight is a very difficult process.

68

28. TODAY'S SERPENTS

Only two of the 23 snakes in Great Smoky Mountains National Park are poisonous. They are the timber rattlesnake and the copperhead. In the Smokies, rattlesnakes rarely are more than four feet long. A few reports of rattlers more than five feet in length have been made. Chipmunks, red squirrels, gray squirrels, cottontails, and mice have been found in the stomachs of many of these snakes.

Hikers may cover hundreds of miles of park trails and not see a single rattlesnake. Yet this type can hardly be thought of as scarce or rare. If you should come across a rattlesnake while hiking in the park, the chances are it will try to get out of your way. If it should hold its ground by coiling and buzzing, you can quickly cause it to quiet down by the use of a fairly long stick. These heavy-bodied, slow-moving serpents do not look for trouble. Danger from snakebite is greatest if you leave the trail in a place where there are rocky outcrops. In that case, be on the alert and watch where you place your feet or your hands.

It is also important to remember that these two kinds of poisonous snakes may be active both day and night during the warmest part of the summer. Hikers should use flashlights or lanterns if walking after dark.

Copperheads, although they do not occur as high in the mountains as rattlesnakes, often are found in the same kinds of places. In fact, the two species are known to hibernate together. A smaller snake than the rattler, the copperhead may be spotted quite easily by the hourglass pattern all along the length of its body. Copperheads are more secretive than rattlesnakes. A favorite hiding place is in old sawdust piles.

The largest of the 21 nonpoisonous snakes in the park are the pilot black snake, black racer, pine snake, common king snake, and corn snake. Of that number, the last three are among our most handsomely marked serpents. The rarest snakes in the park are the mole snake, the black king snake, and the queen snake. The list of Great Smoky Mountains National Park snakes includes the eastern hognose snake, eastern milk snake, rough green snake, common water snake, and common garter snake. The last two are probably the most common types in the area.

Selection 28: Recalling Facts

1. How many varieties of snakes in the park are poisonous?
   ☐ a. Two   ☐ b. Four   ☐ c. Six

2. Rattlesnakes in the Smokies live on
   ☐ a. mice.   ☐ b. bird's eggs.   ☐ c. insects.

3. Rattlesnakes seem to be most common in
   ☐ a. thick grasses.   ☐ b. wooded areas.   ☐ c. rocky places.

4. The author describes rattlesnakes as
   ☐ a. aggressive.   ☐ b. slow-moving.   ☐ c. nonpoisonous.

5. What is the normal maximum length of most rattlesnakes in the park?
   ☐ a. Four feet   ☐ b. Six feet   ☐ c. Eight feet

Selection 28: Understanding Ideas

6. The author implies that poisonous snakes
   ☐ a. are afraid of the dark.
   ☐ b. are most active in warm weather.
   ☐ c. are always searching for food.

7. The reader can assume that copperheads and rattlesnakes
   ☐ a. are mutual friends.
   ☐ b. are bitter enemies.
   ☐ c. are not found together.

8. According to the information presented, copperheads
   ☐ a. live very long lives.
   ☐ b. can be found in swampy areas.
   ☐ c. are easy to recognize.

9. The author points out that the danger of snakebite is lessened
   ☐ a. if the hiker stays on main trails.
   ☐ b. if vehicles are used in camping areas.
   ☐ c. if campers wear colorful clothing.

10. Hikers may cover miles of park trails and not see a single rattlesnake because
    ☐ a. rattlesnakes are scarce in the Smokies.
    ☐ b. rattlesnakes do not look for trouble.
    ☐ c. most people do not know what a rattlesnake looks like.

29. UNIVERSAL FUEL

Wood is our main fuel for fireplaces, stoves, and campfires. It is found in most parts of the world. It is clean and easy to handle. And it is not very expensive. A little knowledge about the best kinds of wood to use, how to lay and start a fire, how to make the fire last for a long time, and how to handle it safely will help you enjoy your outing or get the most out of your fireplace back home.

The conifers are the pines, cedar, spruce, fir, hemlock, and other trees with needlelike leaves. They contain pitch or resins. These trees have wood which burns easily when dry, but the resins or pitch give off a dense smoke. They are good for starting fires and some give off much heat. But they will blacken cooking pans, soot chimneys, and clog stovepipes. Nevertheless, these are widely used and are just about the only type which can be found in some parts of the country.

The broadleaf trees called hardwoods are the oaks, the maple, birch, beech, hickory, gum, poplar, cottonwood, and many others. These do not contain resin and do not give off as much smoke. However, they include very light woods like cottonwood and buckeye and very heavy woods like oak and hickory. There is a great difference in the way that they burn, in the amount of heat they give off, and in the amount of ash they leave. Other features, too, make them desirable or undesirable, such as quick burning, a tendency to throw sparks, or difficulty in igniting them.

A good fire builder knows that he must have tinder, kindling, and fuel, and then fire building is easy.

Tinder can be paper if you're home, but in the outdoors one looks for the dry, dead twigs on the lower part of the trees, dry cedar bark, birch bark even when it's damp, or shavings from the inside of a dry split log. Dead pine needles, leaves, and dry grass can be used for tinder if they are dry.

Kindling is pencil-sized dead twigs broken from trees and the other woody material that breaks rather than bends.

Fuelwood will range in size from as big as a finger to a log 8 to 10 inches in diameter. Logs larger than this may be used in a very large fireplace or where a campfire burns continuously.

Selection 29: Recalling Facts

1. Dead twigs of pencil thickness are called
   - ☐ a. fuelwood.
   - ☐ b. kindling.
   - ☐ c. tinder.

2. Pines, cedars, and spruce are examples of
   - ☐ a. broadleafs.
   - ☐ b. conifers.
   - ☐ c. hardwoods.

3. The disadvantage to burning woods with pitch is that they give off
   - ☐ a. an odor.
   - ☐ b. many sparks.
   - ☐ c. dense smoke.

4. The smallest type of wood used to start fires is called
   - ☐ a. tinder.
   - ☐ b. kindling.
   - ☐ c. fuelwood.

5. Trees with needlelike leaves are called
   - ☐ a. buckeyes.
   - ☐ b. hardwoods.
   - ☐ c. conifers.

Selection 29: Understanding Ideas

6. The author recommends using logs larger than 8 to 10 inches
   - ☐ a. in a stove used for heating.
   - ☐ b. in a campfire that cannot be tended frequently.
   - ☐ c. to start a fire in an indoor fireplace with a good draft.

7. Which one of the following is not true of wood as a fuel?
   - ☐ a. It is relatively inexpensive.
   - ☐ b. It is found almost everywhere.
   - ☐ c. It burns with uniform intensity.

8. The article suggests that the best wood for cooking-fires is
   - ☐ a. any of the conifers.
   - ☐ b. most wood containing resins.
   - ☐ c. hardwoods in general.

9. The intent of this author is
   - ☐ a. to give instructions on using wood as a fuel.
   - ☐ b. to persuade the reader to use wood instead of oil in the home.
   - ☐ c. to convince the reader that a wood shortage does not exist.

10. This selection mostly discusses
    - ☐ a. various shapes of campfires.
    - ☐ b. rules for fire safety.
    - ☐ c. types and sizes of firewood.

30. THE PATHFINDER

When we found him, he was a sorry sight. His clothes were torn, his hands bleeding. Before we reached him, we saw him fall. He lay a moment. Then he pulled himself to his feet, staggered a few yards through the woods and fell again. When we lifted him off the ground, he tried to break away and run, like a wild animal.

After we got him out, we went back to find the gun that he had thrown down. His tracks showed that for two days he had circled in the forest, within 200 yards of the road. His senses were so dulled by fear and exhaustion that he did not hear the cars going by or see the lights at night.

We found him just in time.

This man, like others before him, had simply panicked when he knew he was lost. What had been a near disaster might have turned out as only a pleasant walk, had he taken a few precautions before he stepped from the highway or off a known trail.

Whatever sense of direction that a man may claim, it's still largely a question of observation. Both consciously and subconsciously, a woodsman keeps an eye on his surroundings. He notes the shape of a mountain, the direction water flows through a swamp, and many little traits about every trail he travels—how a tree leans across it, an uprooted stump, a rockslide. He sees the way the ridges run, the general flow of the streams. With these in mind, he may be turned around many times, but he is seldom lost.

There are exceptions, of course, and once in a while a man does get involved in some strange problem that puts him into the "lost" column. A rainstorm or sudden blizzard may catch him without a compass in his pocket. Darkness may find him in a rugged area, where travel is dangerous without a light.

When this happens, the normal first reaction is the dread of embarrassment as a result of his poor woodsmanship. He may also be concerned about the inconvenience that he will cause his friends when he doesn't show up. If he lacks experience, this false pride may lead him to keep on the move in a false effort to find the camp against all odds. He might walk in circles or in the wrong direction and in the end beat himself out physically and mentally.

Selection 30: Recalling Facts

1. How many days had the lost man circled in the forest?
   ☐ a. Two   ☐ b. Four   ☐ c. Six

2. How close had the man been to a road during the time he was lost?
   ☐ a. 100 yards   ☐ b. 200 yards   ☐ c. 300 yards

3. The man did not know that cars were passing by because he was
   ☐ a. exhausted.   ☐ b. blind.   ☐ c. deaf.

4. Finding your way in the woods is largely a question of
   ☐ a. intelligence. ☐ b. observation. ☐ c. endurance.

5. The man is described as a "sorry sight" because of his
   ☐ a. prayerful kneeling. ☐ b. loud crying. ☐ c. bleeding hands.

Selection 30: Understanding Ideas

6. The author suggests that if the man had not been found,
   ☐ a. he would have gone insane.
   ☐ b. he would have run onto the highway.
   ☐ c. he would have been attacked by wild animals.

7. The first thing that the author saw when he found the man was
   ☐ a. the man's torn clothes.
   ☐ b. the remains of a campfire.
   ☐ c. a crude signal for help.

8. After they found the man, they went back to find the man's
   ☐ a. family.   ☐ b. canoe.   ☐ c. weapon.

9. The author tells the story of the lost man as an example of
   ☐ a. people who panic when they think they are lost.
   ☐ b. hunters who go into the woods alone.
   ☐ c. people who do not know how to signal for help properly.

10. According to the article, a good woodsman
    ☐ a. takes notice of wildflowers along the way.
    ☐ b. knows the type of clouds passing overhead.
    ☐ c. tells other people where he is going.

31. THE CHOSEN COUNTRY

Many persons who were born outside of the United States are citizens because they have been naturalized. Millions of people who were born in foreign countries have come to the United States to make their homes. Many of them have done what the law asked them to do in order to become citizens. They have received their citizenship or naturalization papers. They have become naturalized citizens.

The laws that control naturalization are made by the Congress. The Constitution of the United States gives the Congress that power. The Congress passed the Immigration and Nationality Act in 1952. It says that a person can be naturalized only according to the conditions set out in that law.

The law does not let every alien become a citizen. It says, in general, that before he can ask for citizenship he must have reached the age of eighteen years. He must have lived in the United States for at least five years. He must have been present in this country for periods totaling at least half of the five years. He must have been allowed to enter the United States to live here. He must live in the state in which he files his papers for at least six months before he asks for citizenship. Before he can become naturalized, he must be able to speak, read, and write English, if he is physically able to do so. He must understand the history, the Constitution and the government of the United States. He must prove that he has been and is a person of good morals. He cannot be naturalized if, within ten years of the date of filing his petition, he has been against the United States government. He cannot be naturalized if he is or has been a Communist. If an alien has qualified on all matters laid down by the law, then he may be granted citizenship.

Before he can become a citizen, however, the law says that he must take an oath. After the oath has been taken, the judge signs the order allowing naturalization. The new citizen is given a paper of naturalization. This is the official paper that shows that the alien is now a citizen of his new nation, the country of his choice.

Persons interested in becoming naturalized citizens of the United States should apply to the nearest office of the Immigration and Naturalization Service.

Selection 31: Recalling Facts

1. Laws which control naturalization are made by
   ☐ a. the President.   ☐ b. the Congress.   ☐ c. the Secretary of State.

2. The minimum age for citizenship is
   ☐ a. sixteen years.   ☐ b. eighteen years.   ☐ c. twenty-one years.

3. The Immigration and Nationality Act was passed in the early
   ☐ a. 1940s.   ☐ b. 1950s.   ☐ c. 1960s.

4. Before a person can become a citizen, he must
   ☐ a. find a sponsor.   ☐ b. register to vote.   ☐ c. live in America.

5. A person applying for citizenship must take an oath before
   ☐ a. a police officer.   ☐ b. a judge.   ☐ c. a customs official.

Selection 31: Understanding Ideas

6. The author implies that naturalization
   ☐ a. takes many years.
   ☐ b. is automatic with entry to the country.
   ☐ c. cannot be granted to Asians.

7. Before an alien can become a citizen,
   ☐ a he must take courses in American history.
   ☐ b. he must learn the Bill of Rights.
   ☐ c. he must be able to speak English.

8. A naturalized citizen is born
   ☐ a. in the United States to foreign parents.
   ☐ b. to parents who are U.S. citizens.
   ☐ c. in a foreign country.

9. This article discusses
   ☐ a. why people wish to become naturalized citizens.
   ☐ b. the procedure for becoming a naturalized citizen.
   ☐ c. the responsibilities of a naturalized citizen.

10. In this article the author uses the word *petition* to mean
    ☐ a. apply.
    ☐ b. write.
    ☐ c. study.

32. BLACK SNOW

The dark smoke that comes out of stacks or from a burning dump contains tiny bits of solid or liquid matter. The smoke also contains many gases, most of which cannot be seen. Altogether, they make up the serious problems of air pollution. In so many places it keeps us from seeing the sun, irritates our eyes, causes us to cough, or makes us ill.

Air pollution can spread from city to city. It even spreads from one country to another. Some northern European countries have had "black snow" from pollutants that have traveled through the air from other countries and have fallen with the snow. So air pollution is really a global problem.

Air pollution can kill babies, old people and those who have respiratory diseases. In London, in 1952, four thousand people died in one week as a result of a serious air-pollution episode. In 1948, in the small town of Donora, Pennsylvania, twenty people died in a four-day period of bad air pollution.

At levels often found in cities, air pollution increases the risks of certain lung diseases, such as emphysema, bronchitis, and asthma. Of course, smoking and other factors help to cause these illnesses, too, but these cases have increased greatly during recent years as air pollution has become worse.

Air pollution can cause both airplane and auto accidents because it cuts down visibility. There are other possible health dangers from air pollution that we don't know much about. For example, scientists are trying to find out whether chemicals that reach us from the air may cause changes in our cells. These changes might cause babies to be born with serious defects. Scientists are trying to learn how all the many chemicals we are apt to take into our bodies from air, water, food and even medicines act together to affect our health and the way our bodies work. That is another reason why it is so important to begin to control pollution now instead of waiting until we learn all the answers.

Air pollution costs us a lot of money. It soils and corrodes our buildings. It damages farm crops and forests. It has a destructive effect on our works of art. The cost of all this damage in the United States is thought to be more than $16 billion every year. This is far more than the cost of controlling air pollution would be.

Selection 32: Recalling Facts

1. How many people died in London in one week as a result of pollution?
   □ a. 600   □ b. 1,000   □ c. 4,000

2. The author mentions people dying of air pollution in
   □ a. Illinois.   □ b. Pennsylvania.   □ c. New Jersey.

3. According to the author, air pollution increases the incidence of
   □ a. pneumonia.   □ b. hay fever.   □ c. asthma.

4. Air pollution causes airplane accidents because
   □ a. pilots become ill.   □ b. engines fail.   □ c. visibility is reduced.

5. The cost of air pollution damage in the U.S. annually is
   □ a. $16 billion.   □ b. $32 billion.   □ c. $80 billion.

Selection 32: Understanding Ideas

6. Scientists are trying to find a link between pollution and
   □ a. intelligence levels.
   □ b. birth defects.
   □ c. anti-social behavior.

7. "Black snow" is
   □ a. dirty snow.
   □ b. industrial pollution.
   □ c. carbon monoxide.

8. Scientists cannot determine
   □ a. the effects of pollution on the human body.
   □ b. how pollution can be controlled successfully.
   □ c. when the atmosphere first became polluted.

9. The author implies that as air pollution becomes more serious,
   □ a. factories will be forced to stop operating.
   □ b. the earth will begin to grow colder.
   □ c. the government will be forced to investigate the problem.

10. We can conclude that
    □ a. civilization may be doomed if pollution is not controlled.
    □ b. pollution is more serious in Europe than it is in America.
    □ c. most people do not know that pollution is a serious problem.

33. COLOR THEM NEW

What sells cars every year is newness. And what defines "newness" today is color. The cars themselves are "new" each year. But most of what's new is hidden.

One of the most important signals—the thing that tells the consumer at first glance that this is a new car—is color. Twenty years ago, newness was signalled by a set of fins in the showroom. Cars weren't exactly colorful, but they didn't have to be. What the paints lacked in style, the designers made up for with sheet metal and chrome.

That situation has almost been reversed today. It's a reversal that began in the mid-'50s with the use of the "two-tones," especially with the first good "whites" as the second tone.

This is a change that was caused by a lot of things. One of the most important can be summed up in one word—"costs." Costs have helped rule out major body style changes every two years. And the internal changes have added still other costs.

But this glamour isn't something that happened just because somebody's costs went up. It happened because our methods improved. We can make much better finishes now than we could twenty years ago. They're more exciting to see. They last longer. And they're easier to work with on the production line. The result is that we can come up with new colors that will help sell cars.

There isn't any mystery in what colors will sell. There's so much talk about the psychology of color. But it does not really apply in the car-color business. The important thing is a color that the public hasn't seen before, or that it's forgotten.

In the early 1950s, light blue was the most popular. Light and medium greens ran close behind. And one of every ten cars was black.

Ten years later, white had taken over. And from 1959 to 1963, nearly 20 percent of cars were white.

Since then, white has faded in popularity. Today, earth tones have captured the public's interest.

New colors for cars are the product of a complex effort by automobile stylists, researchers developing new pigments, researchers and stylists in the finishes industry, and the people on the production lines.

So the new earth tones were the result of a complex process organized to develop new finishes, finishes that are not only different but tasteful and workable.

Selection 33: Recalling Facts

1. In the sale of cars today, "newness" means
   - ☐ a. styling.
   - ☐ b. performance.
   - ☐ c. color.

2. What factor has ruled out major body-style changes every two years?
   - ☐ a. Production problems
   - ☐ b. Public taste
   - ☐ c. Cost

3. "Two-tones" were first introduced in the middle
   - ☐ a. 1940s.
   - ☐ b. 1950s.
   - ☐ c. 1960s.

4. During the early 1950s the most popular car color was
   - ☐ a. blue.
   - ☐ b. white.
   - ☐ c. black.

5. The most popular colors today are
   - ☐ a. earth tones.
   - ☐ b. two-tones.
   - ☐ c. multi-tones.

Selection 33: Understanding Ideas

6. Twenty years ago, "newness" was indicated by
   - ☐ a. design.
   - ☐ b. horsepower.
   - ☐ c. color.

7. Glamorous cars are mostly the result of
   - ☐ a. the demands of the buying public.
   - ☐ b. the preferences of industry executives.
   - ☐ c. advancements and discoveries in science.

8. Finishes on cars today
   - ☐ a. are more difficult to work with on the assembly line.
   - ☐ b. last longer than they did 20 years ago.
   - ☐ c. require more care than they once did.

9. The "psychology of color"
   - ☐ a. plays an important role in the auto industry.
   - ☐ b. has no bearing on the purchase of cars.
   - ☐ c. is not mentioned in the article.

10. This article does not mention
    - ☐ a. the history of car colors.
    - ☐ b. who is responsible for new colors.
    - ☐ c. color preferences in used cars.

34. HOME, SWEET HOME

An owner should start training his dog as soon as possible after he gets him. A dog will be eager to please his master. Puppies should be about three months old before any training except housebreaking is started. Many organizations and dog clubs give obedience training.

When training a dog, one must never beat him. A slap on the rump or scolding is enough. In obedience training, simple, one-word commands should be used.

Commands should be given in a firm voice. When a dog obeys a command, the master should praise him in a gentle voice and reward him with a few pats on the head. Each obedience lesson should last no longer than fifteen minutes. The master should give several lessons a day.

The first obedience training should be given at home. Then lessons can be given away from home. After awhile, he will learn to obey anywhere in all kinds of situations.

Most dogs can sleep happily inside the home or out. However, sick dogs, old dogs, and short-haired dogs need special housing.

If a dog is to be kept outside, a doghouse and a pen will be needed. The house should be large enough so the dog can turn around inside. It should be small enough so he can keep it warm with his body heat.

The roof must be built over the door of the house to keep out rain and snow. The roof should be removable so the house can be easily cleaned.

The floor of the house should be off the ground so water will not drain into the bedding. A window or shutter is needed for air to come in.

Old clothing, blankets, or some other warm material would make a good bed for him. The bed must be kept dry and clean.

A pen might be 10 to 15 feet long and about 10 feet wide around his house. The owner should use wire fencing high enough so the dog cannot jump over it, and he should bury the bottom edge about 6 inches deep so he cannot dig under it.

Selection 34: Recalling Facts

1. How old should puppies be before training is begun?
   □ a. Six weeks   □ b. One month   □ c. Three months

2. Obedience training should consist of
   □ a. hand movements.
   □ b. sentence commands.
   □ c. one-word commands.

3. The author advises rewarding a puppy with
   □ a. pats on the head.   □ b. bones.   □ c. extra food.

4. Obedience sessions should last no longer than
   □ a. five minutes.   □ b. fifteen minutes.   □ c. one hour.

5. The roof on a doghouse should be
   □ a. shingled.   □ b. insulated.   □ c. removable.

Selection 34: Understanding Ideas

6. Training should begin when a dog is very young because
   □ a. old dogs cannot learn new tricks.
   □ b. young dogs want to please their owners.
   □ c. puppies are afraid of discipline.

7. The author states that praises and commands should be given
   □ a. after the dog is rewarded.
   □ b. along with hand gestures.
   □ c. in different tones of voice.

8. According to the author, obedience training should begin
   □ a. at home.
   □ b. in unfamiliar surroundings.
   □ c. in stress situations.

9. The author implies that
   □ a. German shepherds are easy to train.
   □ b. dogs should be fed once a day.
   □ c. dogs that are kept in pens sometimes dig their way out.

10. From the information provided, we can assume that
    □ a. housebreaking a dog is the first step in obedience training.
    □ b. dogs should not be allowed to sleep inside a house.
    □ c. some breeds of dogs require vitamins with their meals.

35. POLES APART

Many are surprised to learn that Antarctica is nearly twice the size of the United States. The name Antarctica was coined to mean "opposite to the Arctic." It is just that in many ways. Antarctica is a high, ice-covered landmass. In the Arctic the landmasses are grouped around the ice-covered Arctic Ocean.

Largely because of this difference, the climate of the two areas is very different. Antarctica is the coldest area in the world. On the average it is about 30 degrees colder than the Arctic. At the South Pole, nearly 10,000 feet high, monthly mean temperatures run well below zero. Only in coastal regions do temperatures sometimes rise above freezing in the summer (December to March). In contrast, near the North Pole monthly mean temperatures often rise above freezing.

At both poles, daily temperatures may drop far below the monthly mean. At the American South Pole Station, winter temperatures sometimes fall below −100°F. Elsewhere, on higher parts of the south polar plateau, even lower temperatures are recorded. A temperature of −127°F was measured in August 1960. It is the world's record low temperature.

Partly because of this climatic difference, the land animals and plants of the two regions are very different. On the continent of Antarctica, there are very few plants. In the Arctic there are many plants. In some of the few ice-free areas of Antarctica, mosses, lichens, and algae are found. Penguins populate Antarctic coastlines but do not exist in the Arctic. The land animals of the Arctic are foxes, bears, reindeer, and lemmings. These animals are unknown in the Antarctic. Old rock layers show that this "oppositeness" between north and south extends far back into the early chapters of earth history.

Ice is the great feature of Antarctica. More than 4.5 million square miles of ice sheet cover the area. Great rivers of ice, called glaciers, push down the mountains. Antarctica is the storehouse of about 85 percent of the total world supply of ice.

The icecap is very thick, averaging nearly 8,000 feet. At one spot, scientists have found the distance from the surface to the rock underneath the ice to be more than 13,000 feet.

If this great volume of ice were to melt, the volume of the world oceans would increase, and sea level would rise.

Selection 35: Recalling Facts

1. The coldest area in the world is
   □ a. the Arctic.   □ b. Antarctica.   □ c. Siberia.

2. The world's record low temperature was recorded in
   □ a. 1950.   □ b. 1960.   □ c. 1970.

3. How much of the world's ice is located at Antarctica?
   □ a. 15 percent   □ b. 55 percent   □ c. 85 percent

4. Compared to the United States, Antarctica is
   □ a. the same size.   □ b. twice the size.   □ c. four times the size.

5. Some areas of Antarctica are
   □ a. ice-free.   □ b. very humid.   □ c. quite mild.

Selection 35: Understanding Ideas

6. One type of animal found in the Arctic is
   □ a. the fox.   □ b. the wolf.   □ c. the opossum.

7. The author develops his point through
   □ a. comparison and contrast.
   □ b. theories and proof.
   □ c. characters and actions.

8. The author implies that if Antarctica's ice melted,
   □ a. coastal areas of the world would be flooded.
   □ b. ocean currents would shift direction.
   □ c. climate would change drastically everywhere.

9. The name Antarctica, meaning "opposite to the Arctic," was based on
   □ a. insufficient exploration.
   □ b. inaccurate information.
   □ c. adequate knowledge.

10. We may conclude that
    □ a. life at the North Pole is more tolerable than at the South Pole.
    □ b. the Arctic is a solid land mass.
    □ c. penguins could not live at the North Pole.

36. THE AMERICAN VOTER

Democracy is a way of life. Like other living things, it needs care. To keep democracy alive in the United States, every citizen must do his share to protect it. Voting in elections is one of the important ways of protecting democracy. When they vote, the citizens help express the will of the people. It is not only the right of every American citizen to vote, but it is also his responsibility.

Voting, in itself, is not enough. If we are to have leaders who will give us good government, we must choose them wisely. Every voter should learn all he can about the candidates and the issues in an election. He should know why he is for or against a candidate or an issue.

A good citizen does not vote one way or another just to please a friend or neighbor. The intelligent voter thinks for himself and makes his own decision. His vote is secret.

There are many ways in which a voter can learn about the candidates and the issues. He can listen to persons who are helping the candidate to win the election. These people tell what the candidate promises to do for the citizens if they elect him. The voter can also attend meetings and hear the candidate himself.

Information about candidates and issues is given in newspapers, magazines and books. Circulars and pamphlets sent to the homes of voters by political parties are other sources of information.

The intelligent voter can also get information in his own home. Members of the family can talk about what they have learned and what they think. The same thing can be done at the place where the voter works.

The voter should learn what is said for each candidate and issue, as well as what is said against them. It would be foolish for him to believe everything that he hears and reads. By learning about each side, the voter can compare the information and then make up his own mind. This is the intelligent way of keeping democracy alive.

The duty of a good citizen does not end with voting. After the election is over, a voter should make sure that the person who was elected is doing what he promised he would do. He may not be keeping his promises. When this happens, the voters have a duty to elect a better person at the next election.

Selection 36: Recalling Facts

1. The author describes democracy as
   - ☐ a. the oldest form of government.
   - ☐ b. a blessing for the poor.
   - ☐ c. a living thing.

2. One way to protect democracy is
   - ☐ a. to hold office.
   - ☐ b. to vote.
   - ☐ c. to save money.

3. The author does not mention advertising
   - ☐ a. on television.
   - ☐ b. in newspapers.
   - ☐ c. in books.

4. A good citizen votes in elections to please
   - ☐ a. his family.
   - ☐ b. his friends.
   - ☐ c. himself.

5. The author feels that members of a family
   - ☐ a. should vote differently.
   - ☐ b. should discuss candidates.
   - ☐ c. should avoid discussing politics.

Selection 36: Understanding Ideas

6. According to the author, people should vote for
   - ☐ a. friends and relatives.
   - ☐ b. people whom they have met personally.
   - ☐ c. people who are most qualified.

7. People who help candidates to win elections usually
   - ☐ a. provide important information for voters.
   - ☐ b. make false and misleading statements.
   - ☐ c. cause candidates to lose many friends.

8. The author states that some political parties
   - ☐ a. send pamphlets.
   - ☐ b. debate in public.
   - ☐ c. spend money foolishly.

9. The author advises the voter
   - ☐ a. to keep his views a secret.
   - ☐ b. to discuss political issues at work.
   - ☐ c. to campaign for at least one politician.

10. We can conclude that
    - ☐ a. an informed citizen is an intelligent voter.
    - ☐ b. most people vote without knowing the issues.
    - ☐ c. some politicians are elected by mistake.

37. NOT A DROP TO DRINK

A few years ago, most streams and lakes in America were sparkling and clean. People could swim and fish in them without becoming sick. But as the nation grew bigger, we built towns and factories on the banks of these streams and lakes. Every year we dumped more and more wastes into our waters. People thought that the water would carry the wastes away and purify itself. This was true when the amount of wastes was small. But as our population has grown, the greater amounts of wastes have not been well handled.

What we have done is to overload the water recycling system of the earth. Now most of our streams and lakes show signs of man's abuse. Many are very polluted. The Cuyahoga River in Ohio, for example, had so much rubble and oil in it that it actually caught fire a few years ago.

One of our beautiful Great Lakes, Lake Erie, is in serious trouble as a result of aging. This is a natural process for all bodies of water, but it is speeded up by man's pollution. Certain pollutants make plants grow too fast and disturb the plant growth balance of the lake. Scientists say that pollution has aged Lake Erie many years in a very short time. To save it, we must stop dumping wastes into the lake and take strong action to clean it up.

Marine scientists have found that even the ocean depths show the effects of pollution. And in shallower waters near our coasts, pollution prevents the harvesting of fish and shellfish in many areas. Oil, spilled by accident or even dumped on purpose in the ocean, has become a big problem because it spoils our beaches and kills fish and sea birds.

The water that we drink is normally taken from the best and cleanest sources, then treated to make sure it is safe for drinking. But with so much pollution, it is harder to find good water. Even water far below the ground, from which many cities get their drinking water, is sometimes polluted by poisonous wastes flowing into the soil.

More than 1,416 towns let their sewage flow into waters without any treatment whatever. Sewage wastes in the United States are expected to increase by nearly four times in the next fifty years. It is very important to build better, more advanced sewage treatment plants that can take out almost all pollution.

Selection 37: Recalling Facts

1. The river mentioned is located in
   - ☐ a. Texas.
   - ☐ b. Missouri.
   - ☐ c. Ohio.

2. The lake which is in serious trouble because of aging is
   - ☐ a. Lake Ontario.
   - ☐ b. Lake Erie.
   - ☐ c. Lake Michigan.

3. How many communities discharge untreated sewage into waterways?
   - ☐ a. Fewer than 500
   - ☐ b. More than 1,000
   - ☐ c. Nearly 3,000

4. The author mentions one polluted river which
   - ☐ a. turned black.
   - ☐ b. caught fire.
   - ☐ c. caused disease.

5. During the next 50 years, sewage wastes in the U.S. are expected
   - ☐ a. to increase three times.
   - ☐ b. to increase four times.
   - ☐ c. to increase five times.

Selection 37: Understanding Ideas

6. This article is primarily about
   - ☐ a. waste systems used by industries.
   - ☐ b. the dangers of polluted water.
   - ☐ c. the work of marine scientists.

7. Not too long ago, people thought that pollutants in streams
   - ☐ a. were carried eventually out to sea.
   - ☐ b. dissolved and disappeared.
   - ☐ c. were absorbed by plants growing underwater.

8. The author is hopeful that
   - ☐ a. large companies will be fined for polluting streams.
   - ☐ b. communities will find sources of clean drinking water.
   - ☐ c. better sewage treatment plants will be built.

9. The author feels that pollution has become a serious problem
   - ☐ a. because the population has increased rapidly.
   - ☐ b. because the government has been indifferent to the situation.
   - ☐ c. because factories now use more chemicals than they once did.

10. We can conclude that
    - ☐ a. no clean water can be found anywhere.
    - ☐ b. pollution is difficult to control.
    - ☐ c. pollution laws are too strict.

38. BODY BUILDERS

All life needs protein. It is the main tissue builder. It is the basic substance of every cell in the body.

Protein is made up of smaller units called amino acids. After foods are eaten, the proteins are broken down into amino acids. They are then rearranged to form the many special proteins in the body.

The proteins in food are made up of eighteen or more amino acids. The body can make its own supply of more than half of these. But the others must come from food and are called essential amino acids.

The amount of amino acid in a food protein shows its food value. Proteins that supply all the essential amino acids are highest in value. Foods that have large amounts of these good proteins best meet the body's needs. Generally, these are foods from animals like meat, fish, poultry, eggs, and milk.

Proteins from cereal grains, vegetables, and fruits do not have as many kinds of amino acids as animal proteins do, but they do supply valuable amounts of many amino acids. Proteins from legumes, especially soybeans, chickpeas, and peanuts, are almost as good as proteins from animal sources.

Large amounts of protein are found in meat, poultry, fish, milk, cheese, eggs, dry beans, dry peas, and nuts. Bread, cereals, vegetables, and fruits have smaller amounts of protein. However, the amount of bread eaten daily may be large enough to make these foods good sources.

To have daily meals rank well in protein quality, only a part of the protein has to come from animal sources. Combining cereals and vegetables with a little meat or other source of animal protein will improve the protein value of the meal. Examples of nourishing combinations are cereal with milk, rice with fish, spaghetti with meat sauce, or vegetable stew with meat. Milk along with foods of plant origin is also nourishing. It is a good idea to have some food from animal sources at each meal.

Protein is necessary all through life for the maintenance and repair of body tissues. Children need protein for normal growth.

Building of cells is only one of the jobs of protein. Among other functions, protein helps to make hemoglobin. This is the blood protein that carries oxygen to the cells and carries carbon dioxide away from them. Protein helps to form antibodies that fight infection. Protein also supplies energy.

Selection 38: Recalling Facts

1. How many amino acids do proteins contain?
   ☐ a. Nine   ☐ b. Thirteen   ☐ c. Eighteen

2. Essential amino acids come from
   ☐ a. food.   ☐ b. the body.   ☐ c. vitamins.

3. The highest amounts of amino acids are found in
   ☐ a. vegetables.   ☐ b. cereal grains.   ☐ c. poultry.

4. According to the author, protein helps people to
   ☐ a. relax.   ☐ b. fight infection.   ☐ c. think.

5. The nutritive value of food proteins is determined by
   ☐ a. calories.   ☐ b. amino acids.   ☐ c. metabolism.

Selection 38: Understanding Ideas

6. The author states that
   ☐ a. the body can manufacture nine amino acids.
   ☐ b. sugar does not contain any protein.
   ☐ c. some people are unable to absorb protein.

7. In this article, the author stresses the need for
   ☐ a. a high-protein breakfast each day.
   ☐ b. animal protein at each meal.
   ☐ c. substituting vegetable protein for meat protein.

8. The author mentions a meal of spaghetti with meat sauce
   ☐ a. as an example of a poorly balanced meal.
   ☐ b. as an illustration of a meal high in starch.
   ☐ c. as a sample of a nourishing meal.

9. This article is probably from
   ☐ a. a doctoral thesis on the structure of protein.
   ☐ b. a magazine on nutrition.
   ☐ c. a technical journal on body chemistry.

10. We can conclude that
    ☐ a. vegetarians are basically unhealthy people.
    ☐ b. some foods are richer sources of protein than others.
    ☐ c. children need more protein than adults.

39. A LIVING LINK

In a land with a story as old as that of Britain, the past is an important part of the people's way of life. The Royal Family is a living link with the kings and the tales of the past. To the British, Queen Elizabeth II is a symbol of Britain's unity. Wherever and whenever she appears, she is given respect and warm feelings.

Many of the old customs which are part of this respect for the Royal Family are still followed today.

Even in this modern age the Monarch's Champion can be seen in the parade held when a new ruler takes the throne. The Champion's role now is to carry the royal flag. Up until 200 years ago the knight who had this title rode his horse into the banquet hall where the new king was dining. There he shouted out a challenge to fight anyone who did not believe that the new king was the rightful heir to the throne.

In late October or early November the Queen personally takes part in another old and colorful ceremony. This is the Opening of Parliament. From Buckingham Palace to the Parliament, thousands of Britons line the streets to see their ruler pass in a horse-drawn carriage.

Another old ceremony, Trooping the Colour, takes place in London in early June. It is also called the Queen's Birthday Parade since it marks the official birthday of the ruler. This is an important military event. It is a time when the Queen inspects units of the Brigade of Guards.

Some of the British customs are not related to the life of the Royal Family.

A yearly event with an old beginning is Guy Fawkes Day, November 5. This marks the day in 1605 on which Fawkes tried to blow up the Parliament buildings. Now, weeks before the event, in every part of the United Kingdom children carry a homemade, stuffed likeness of Fawkes and ask for "a penny for the Guy." the money they collect is spent for fireworks and candy.

Only a few days later is the City of London's finest show. This is the day when the elected Lord Mayor of the City of London takes office. For the event the Lord Mayor is carried from the Guildhall to the law courts in a horse-drawn coach. There he is met by an agent of the ruler and his election is made official.

Selection 39: Recalling Facts

1. To the British, Queen Elizabeth represents
   ☐ a. tradition. ☐ b. courage. ☐ c. unity.

2. The role of the Monarch's Champion is to carry
   ☐ a. a flag. ☐ b. a crown. ☐ c. a sword.

3. The Opening of Parliament occurs in
   ☐ a. spring. ☐ b. summer. ☐ c. fall.

4. Guy Fawkes became famous during the early
   ☐ a. 1500s. ☐ b. 1600s. ☐ c. 1700s.

5. The Queen inspects units of the Brigade of Guards
   ☐ a. during the Queen's Birthday Parade.
   ☐ b. on Guy Fawkes Day.
   ☐ c. during the Opening of Parliament.

Selection 39: Understanding Ideas

6. The original role of the Monarch's Champion was
   ☐ a. to slay the enemy in combat.
   ☐ b. to defend the rights of the king.
   ☐ c. to predict the future for royalty.

7. The title, "A Living Link," refers to
   ☐ a. the continuation of the Royal Family.
   ☐ b. scientific discoveries in the origins of man.
   ☐ c. research in animal behavior.

8. In English history Guy Fawkes was
   ☐ a. a hero.
   ☐ b. a criminal.
   ☐ c. a member of royalty.

9. Guy Fawkes Day is similar to the American
   ☐ a. Christmas.
   ☐ b. Thanksgiving.
   ☐ c. Halloween.

10. The Lord Mayor of London
    ☐ a. is the most powerful figure in England.
    ☐ b. is always related to the Royal Family.
    ☐ c. takes office in November.

40. COSMETICS

A few cosmetics being sold today are called hypo-allergenic. This label means that they can be used by a large number of people who may be allergic to other cosmetics.

However, just because a company says that a product is hypo-allergenic does not make it so. The idea of hypo-allergenic cosmetics is so unclear that it does not give any real protection for the user.

If you have allergies, the best way to make sure you are buying a cosmetic which you can use safely is to buy small amounts at first. Test the product. Use a little of it on your arm. If it causes a problem, then you know you shouldn't buy any more.

Cosmetics are generally safe if used according to the instructions on the label. But cosmetics, like any other product, can be harmful if they are not used right.

Before using any cosmetic, read the label carefully and follow directions exactly. This is very important when using antiperspirants, hair-removing products, hair dyes and colors, home permanents, and skin packs.

To see if you are allergic to a cosmetic, apply a small amount on the inside of your forearm. Leave it for 24 hours. If you notice any redness or blisters, don't use it again. In the case of hair preparations, do a patch test. Use it as directed on one small area of the hair and scalp to see whether there is a problem before using it for the entire area.

If a cosmetic causes any burning, breaking out, stinging, or itching, stop using it. If the condition seems to be serious, see your doctor.

Report any problems to the company that makes the product and to the FDA. You will be doing a public service.

Don't let children play with cosmetics. Keep cosmetics out of their reach.

Be very careful using eye cosmetics to avoid possible damage to the eyes.

Cosmetics are very important to our well-being. When we feel attractive, we feel accepted and secure.

But cosmetics cannot change us permanently. They cannot keep us young or healthy, or grow hair on bald heads, or prevent wrinkles.

When you're buying cosmetics, keep in mind that they are made to bring out your good features or cover up some flaws. But they cannot make you over, nor can they assure your living happily ever after.

Selection 40: Recalling Facts

1. The concept of hypo-allergenic cosmetics is
   - ☐ a. precise.
   - ☐ b. misleading.
   - ☐ c. vague.

2. It is very important to follow label instructions for
   - ☐ a. nail polishes.
   - ☐ b. antiperspirants.
   - ☐ c. hand creams.

3. To test a cosmetic for safety, one should leave it on the skin for
   - ☐ a. 6 hours.
   - ☐ b. 12 hours.
   - ☐ c. 24 hours.

4. A patch test is a good way to test
   - ☐ a. hair colors.
   - ☐ b. lipsticks.
   - ☐ c. powders.

5. Adverse effects from cosmetics can be reported to the
   - ☐ a. Attorney General.
   - ☐ b. FDA.
   - ☐ c. Congress.

Selection 40: Understanding Ideas

6. The author points out that cosmetics
   - ☐ a. can cause blindness.
   - ☐ b. improve our self-image.
   - ☐ c. are unnecessary for men.

7. The author warns that cosmetics cannot
   - ☐ a. improve a person's health.
   - ☐ b. make us feel attractive.
   - ☐ c. enhance a person's good features.

8. In writing this passage, the author uses
   - ☐ a. limited facts.
   - ☐ b. interesting interviews.
   - ☐ c. excellent comparisons.

9. The author is concerned mostly with
   - ☐ a. specially formulated cosmetics.
   - ☐ b. cosmetics in general.
   - ☐ c. the use of imported cosmetics.

10. Cosmetics present a threat to a person's health because of their
   - ☐ a. application.
   - ☐ b. ingredients.
   - ☐ c. overuse.

41. CIVIL RIGHTS OF AMERICANS

All Americans have certain rights under the U.S. Constitution and federal laws. These rights protect you against unfair acts by government officials and private individuals.

It is up to you to use your rights. If you don't know what your rights are, ask for help from a lawyer. If you cannot pay a lawyer, one will be hired for you in most criminal cases. If you do not have a criminal case, you may be able to get help from a legal assistance program. You can find a legal assistance program by looking in your phone book or by calling the local bar (lawyers') association.

You have the right to believe what you wish and to state your beliefs in speech or in print. The rights to free speech and press are protected by the first amendment to the United States Constitution.

No government official at the federal, state, or local level can punish you for your beliefs or for stating them to others. You have the right to freely join together with others in social, political, or religious groups, such as political parties and churches. The government can make rules about when, where, and how you or your group may speak out in public, but these rules must be reasonable.

The federal and state governments cannot favor any one religious group over another. They cannot cut off any government services because you say what your beliefs are. You are free to choose your own religion or faith. Or, if you want to, you can decide not to have any religious belief at all.

An important right is your right to "petition for a redress of grievance." What this means is that you can freely tell your government officials about any problems that bother you.

Adult citizens have the right to register to vote, join political parties, and vote. They can run for office in all elections on the federal, state, and local level. No one can charge you a fee, make you pay a poll tax, make you take a literacy test or make you speak or read English in order to vote. Elections must be held fairly, and all votes must be counted equally. If someone threatens you or tries to take away your rights to register and vote, report it to the Assistant Attorney General, Civil Rights Division, Department of Justice, Washington, D.C.

Selection 41: Recalling Facts

1. The article says that to learn what your rights are, ask
   □ a. a lawyer. □ b. a Congressman. □ c. a state official.

2. Which amendment protects a person's rights to free speech?
   □ a. First □ b. Fifth □ c. Tenth

3. The document which gives Americans certain rights is
   □ a. the Declaration of Independence.
   □ b. the Constitution.
   □ c. the Rights of Redress.

4. A bar association is a group of
   □ a. lawyers. □ b. judges. □ c. city officials.

5. If someone stops you from voting, you can report it to the Department of
   □ a. Defense. □ b. Justice. □ c. State.

Selection 41: Understanding Ideas

6. This selection is mostly about
   □ a. United States documents.
   □ b. legal restrictions on Americans.
   □ c. civil rights for Americans.

7. If you are unable to pay a private lawyer's fees,
   □ a. the court will provide a lawyer free of charge.
   □ b. the lawyer will often reduce his fees to meet your ability.
   □ c. the court may refuse to hear your case temporarily.

8. In regard to speaking out in public, the government may
   □ a. tell you that you cannot speak on the steps of the state capitol.
   □ b. prohibit you from speaking against certain politicians.
   □ c. arrest you for publicly approving of foreign governments.

9. Under a "petition for a redress of grievance," you should
   □ a. write to a lawyer for assistance.
   □ b. contact your state senator.
   □ c. demand that you be heard in the Court of Appeals.

10. In order to vote in any election, you must know
    □ a. how to pay a poll tax.
    □ b. when an election is being held.
    □ c. where an intelligence test is being given.

42. HIKING

Hiking is not only one of the best forms of physical exercise, but one of the best forms of mental diversion too. It is both relaxing and stimulating. It is good for all ages and especially good as a family and group activity.

Since hiking varies so widely in the distance covered and the types of trails and terrains, it is not possible to give any general rules to follow. Short and frequent hikes, needing no planning or special equipment, are enjoyed by most people.

• Keep in shape by walking at a fast pace for at least 15 minutes every day. Climbing stairs instead of using an elevator and running short distances are also good ways of keeping in shape.

• Wear only comfortable clothing. And when you are hiking in the mountains or in areas subject to sudden changes in the weather, take a windbreaker, a sweater, or other protection against cold and rain.

Two pairs of socks, one thin and one thick, should be worn on long hikes.

• On any hike nothing is more important than good, comfortable shoes.

• The things you take might include matches in a waterproof box, a knife, compass, map, bandages or other first aid items, insect repellent, and a flashlight.

• Food can vary from a box of raisins on a short hike to dehydrated meals cooked over a small stove during a long hike.

• Binoculars or cameras may be taken, but don't overload with too much gear.

• On longer hikes keep a comfortable, steady pace and take rest stops often.

• Drink only safe water. If in doubt, boil the water or use purification tablets.

• Avoid the busy roads. When you have to use a road, keep as far over on the left as possible.

• Leave word at home or some other place where you are going and when you plan to be back.

• On almost any hike, a map is a good idea. If going into strange country, a detailed map showing contours and landmarks is most helpful.

• Take along a field guide on flowers, birds, rocks, or other subjects depending upon your interests. This can add greatly to the enjoyment and educational value of your hike.

Much of the most beautiful scenery lies hidden away from the main roads. How much more fun it is to get out of your car and enjoy the fun and exercise of a hike in the outdoors!

Selection 42: Recalling Facts

1. The author recommends keeping in shape with a daily walk of
   □ a. 15 minutes.   □ b. 30 minutes.   □ c. 45 minutes.

2. The author feels that the most essential item on a hike is
   □ a. a new map.   □ b. outdoor tools.   □ c. good shoes.

3. The best snack for a short hike is
   □ a. beans.   □ b. crackers.   □ c. raisins.

4. When you have to walk on a highway, keep to the
   □ a. right.   □ b. left.   □ c. middle.

5. The author says that hiking is especially valuable for
   □ a. individuals.   □ b. families.   □ c. retirees.

Selection 42: Understanding Ideas

6. This article is about hiking as
   □ a. a competitive sport.
   □ b. a leisurely pastime.
   □ c. a strenuous activity.

7. The article implies that hiking is
   □ a. a relaxing form of exercise.
   □ b. a dangerous activity for older people.
   □ c. not as popular as it was once.

8. The author of this selection is mostly concerned with
   □ a. general rules for hiking in mountainous areas.
   □ b. precautions to be taken against dangerous animals.
   □ c. general procedures to follow in hiking.

9. The author recommends
   □ a. leaving binoculars and cameras at home.
   □ b. drinking water from streams only.
   □ c. avoiding highways.

10. To develop his main idea the author uses
    □ a. arguments.
    □ b. suggestions.
    □ c. comparisons.

43. PARADE OF PESTS

Many pests that invade homes are present at all times in all parts of the United States. Some are found only at certain times or in certain areas.

Many kinds of ants invade homes. Some ants have wings. Termites quickly shed their wings soon after they enter a building. Thus, ants are often mistaken for termites.

The two insects, however, are very different in appearance. Ants are "pinched in" at the waistline. Termites have no "pinching in" at the waistline. Also, the rear wings of an ant are much smaller than the front wings. They often are attached to them. But there is little difference in size between the rear and front wings of a termite.

Ants crawl over any food they can reach. They spoil it for humans and carry bits of it to their nests.

They usually do not attack fabrics, leather, or similar materials found in homes. They seldom attack very sound wood, but some kinds damage old wooden structures. They make their nests in the rotting woodwork.

The ants' nest may be outdoors or it may be within a wall in the house. The nest may be under flooring, under a pile of papers, or in an out-of-the-way corner. Sometimes it is possible to trace the ants' line of march from the food source to the location of the nest.

If the nest is found, it should be treated with insecticide. If the nest is outdoors, all cracks and openings into the house through which the ants might enter should be sealed off.

For most places, an insecticide can be applied as a surface spray. For kitchen treatments, the liquid can be applied with a small paintbrush.

Insecticide must be applied to surfaces over which the ants crawl in their line of march. All cracks, openings, or runways which they may be using to enter the house must be treated. These may include the lower part of window frames; around doors, supports, posts, pillars, or pipes that the ants might use as runways into the house; cracks in baseboards, walls, and floors; and openings around electrical outlets and plumbing or heating pipes.

It will take a few days for the ants to reach the insecticide deposits. If the pests continue to appear, they probably are using surfaces which have not been treated. Then those surfaces must be treated.

Selection 43: Recalling Facts

1. Termites shed their wings soon after they
   - ☐ a. become adults.
   - ☐ b. breed.
   - ☐ c. enter a building.

2. Ants usually do not eat or destroy
   - ☐ a. wood.
   - ☐ b. leather.
   - ☐ c. garbage.

3. Insecticides are used
   - ☐ a. to protect food.
   - ☐ b. to kill bugs.
   - ☐ c. to seal cracks.

4. Insects often enter the living quarters of a house
   - ☐ a. on clothes.
   - ☐ b. in groceries.
   - ☐ c. through electrical boxes.

5. The rear wings of some ants
   - ☐ a. are larger than the front wings.
   - ☐ b. are smaller than the front wings.
   - ☐ c. are often the same size as the front wings.

Selection 43: Understanding Ideas

6. According to the author,
   - ☐ a. ants are members of the termite family.
   - ☐ b. ants are really a kind of termite.
   - ☐ c. ants are often mistaken for termites.

7. The article suggests that
   - ☐ a. termites are more destructive than ants.
   - ☐ b. termites often carry food from the kitchen area.
   - ☐ c. termites are much larger than ants.

8. In this article, the author is concerned primarily with
   - ☐ a. protection from ants.
   - ☐ b. the habits of termites.
   - ☐ c. the use of pesticides.

9. The author states that
   - ☐ a. ants sometimes build their nests outside.
   - ☐ b. termites breed more rapidly than ants.
   - ☐ c. termites make tunnels in the wood they attack.

10. The reader can conclude that
    - ☐ a. insects are man's greatest natural enemy.
    - ☐ b. insect damage is often more obvious than the insects themselves.
    - ☐ c. insects are usually afraid of sunlight.

44. A BODY WITHOUT A HEAD

Soon after the Declaration of Independence was signed, the Continental Congress drew up a plan for a central government. The plan was called The *Articles of Confederation and Perpetual Union.* It was sent to the states. They were asked to accept it.

Many of the states did not like the plan. Some said that the central government would not be strong enough. Other states feared that they would lose the right to govern their own people. Changes were made in the plan. It was accepted by all of the thirteen states by March 1, 1781.

Under the Articles of Confederation, the states entered into "a firm league of friendship" with one another. The people in each state thought of the other states as friends. They would help one another. But the people did not think that they were members of a true Union.

The Articles of Confederation set up a Congress of one House only. Each state was represented in that House. Each state had only one vote.

The Congress had power to make war and peace. It could make money. A committee of the Congress governed the nation when the Congress was not meeting.

After the war was won, the purpose in working together was gone. The war had held the states together to win freedom. Many of the people thought that the Union had ended. The states fought with one another.

The central government did not have enough power to carry on its work. The Congress could do nothing unless the states agreed. For example, the Congress asked the states for money, but could not force them to pay. The Congress could not tax the citizens. The Congress asked the states to send soldiers to protect the nation. But some of the states refused. The Congress made treaties with other countries. But the states did not obey the treaties.

The Articles of Confederation were weak in other ways. There was no President. The central government was "a body without a head." There were no federal courts. The Congress could not force any person to obey the laws.

The Congress had no power to control trade among the states or between the states and foreign countries. The states fought over the right to tax goods from other states. Also, the states fought over the ownership of certain lands. Virginia and Maryland could not agree about which state owned Chesapeake Bay.

Selection 44: Recalling Facts

1. How many states accepted the Articles of Confederation?
   - ☐ a. Nine
   - ☐ b. Thirteen
   - ☐ c. Fifteen

2. The Articles of Confederation was accepted in the year
   - ☐ a. 1776.
   - ☐ b. 1781.
   - ☐ c. 1812.

3. In Congress, each state was given
   - ☐ a. one vote.
   - ☐ b. two votes.
   - ☐ c. three votes.

4. The author mentions the state of
   - ☐ a. Florida.
   - ☐ b. Maine.
   - ☐ c. Virginia.

5. The Articles of Confederation were drawn up by
   - ☐ a. the President.
   - ☐ b. the Continental Congress.
   - ☐ c. the New England states.

Selection 44: Understanding Ideas

6. Under the Articles of Confederation, the government could
   - ☐ a. set up a postal department.
   - ☐ b. set up a welfare department.
   - ☐ c. set up a treasury department.

7. Just after the Articles of Confederation was accepted,
   - ☐ a. the United States waged war on England.
   - ☐ b. a President was elected.
   - ☐ c. the states began to argue among themselves.

8. One drawback to the Articles of Confederation was that
   - ☐ a. it did not create courts.
   - ☐ b. it did not allow Congress to declare war.
   - ☐ c. it did not allow Congress to ask states for money.

9. The phrase "body without a head" means
   - ☐ a. a state without a capital.
   - ☐ b. a senator without power.
   - ☐ c. a government without a President.

10. The Articles of Confederation was written
    - ☐ a. before the Declaration of Independence was signed.
    - ☐ b. during the Revolutionary War.
    - ☐ c. after the Declaration of Independence was signed.

45. ROME UNDER WRAPS

The tourist crush is over in Rome. The *Closed for Vacation* signs of late summer have been put away for another year.

The Romans themselves come back home in September after warm, restful months at the beaches. The city opens up. Sidewalk cafés by the hundreds are back in business, each with its own post-holiday specialties.

The foreign crowds have gone. It's now a Rome for the Romans.

A stroll along the Via Margutta, near Piazza di Spagna where the Spanish Steps are located, finds the throngs of tourists gone. Instead, traveling artists and writers visit the area. All over Rome art galleries are having openings for the fall season. Sounds of English, German, and French are heard.

Rome is in its fullest glory in the autumn. Its people are tanned, airy, and happier than usual. Top restaurants in Trastevere, the colorful old section across the Tiber, and elsewhere in the city are again in full swing, along with the discotheques and nightclubs.

At outdoor restaurants in the evenings, the rich forget they are rich, and the poor forget they are poor. Tables are heavy with food and wine. People talk, laugh, and sing with their neighbors. The traveler will find language no problem, especially after the first glass of wine together. The Romans will use any manner to express themselves.

It's an ideal time to visit the always-green Tivoli and Borghese gardens and the ruins of ancient Rome. For the most part, they're quiet after the summer season. This is the best time to get the feel of that centuries-old civilization. Visiting Rome in the quiet season also gives time for quick side-trips to Naples, Capri, and Florence.

It's pleasant weather, too; just cool enough for a light coat. When November comes, the temperature starts to dip, and until the end of February an overcoat is needed. If by some chance it does snow at all, it melts almost immediately. Warm winds off the African desert can bring mild weather on many winter days.

The real joy of Rome's winter is the Christmas season. The marvelous Sistine Chapel Choir and the Pontifical Superior School of Sacred Music can be seen and heard. Practically every basilica, church, or chapel welcomes worshipers with a chorus of majestic music and Gregorian chants.

Selection 45: Recalling Facts

1. The Spanish Steps are noted for their
   - ☐ a. pigeons.
   - ☐ b. artists.
   - ☐ c. restaurants.

2. Romans seem happiest during
   - ☐ a. spring.
   - ☐ b. summer.
   - ☐ c. autumn.

3. Famous gardens are located in
   - ☐ a. Naples.
   - ☐ b. Capri.
   - ☐ c. Tivoli.

4. Rome is often warmed in winter by winds from
   - ☐ a. eastern Spain.
   - ☐ b. the African desert.
   - ☐ c. the Swiss Alps.

5. During the winter months, a resident of Rome would not find many
   - ☐ a. open restaurants.
   - ☐ b. foreign tourists.
   - ☐ c. green gardens.

Selection 45: Understanding Ideas

6. The author states that snow in Rome is
   - ☐ a. unheard-of.
   - ☐ b. very rare.
   - ☐ c. quite common.

7. This article is probably from
   - ☐ a. a travel brochure.
   - ☐ b. a history book.
   - ☐ c. a report about European customs.

8. The author implies that
   - ☐ a. Naples is located near Rome.
   - ☐ b. Florence is a small island.
   - ☐ c. Rome is located in northern Italy.

9. The author is enthusiastic about
   - ☐ a. the ancient ruins of Rome.
   - ☐ b. the Christmas season in Rome.
   - ☐ c. the art museums in Rome.

10. We can conclude that
    - ☐ a. Rome is a pleasant place to visit in winter.
    - ☐ b. Rome is very expensive to visit in the fall.
    - ☐ c. Rome is crowded during the spring months.

46. EARLY GROUPS

Many people have come to the United States during the past 350 years. They came from many different countries. Some of the people came long ago. Others have come more recently. The people who came long ago always came in groups.

The first groups came to explore. They went home and told the people about the good earth, the new fruits, and the Indians in the new country. Other persons decided to explore it. Later this new country was named America.

Some of the people who heard about America had not been happy for a long time. They were not allowed to worship God as they pleased. Their government set up a church for them. They refused to join the church, but they had to pay taxes to help support it. Some of the people had even moved to other countries. But still they were not free enough to be happy.

In some countries, the people could not write or speak openly. The government officers stopped them. In other countries, the people had to pay taxes but could not say how the taxes should be spent. Also, the officers often put people in prison without telling them what crimes they were accused of having committed.

Some of the groups wanted to set up their own government. They were not happy in their homelands. They decided to cross the ocean and to build new homes in America. They hoped to be free.

The early groups of people who came to America were different in many ways. For example, they wore different kinds of clothes. They spoke different languages. They had different ways of worshipping God. The Roman Catholics in Maryland had one form of worship. The Pilgrims in Massachusetts had another form. And the Quakers in Pennsylvania had still another form of worship.

But the groups were like one another in many ways. For example, all of the groups belived in God, although they used different prayers. All of the groups had come to America for a purpose. Each group gave authority to a few men to make rules or laws for the group. The people in each group chose other men to enforce the laws of the group.

The groups soon learned to live better by helping each other. Small groups came together in towns and built walls to protect their people from enemies. They also learned to help each other by making their groups larger.

Selection 46: Recalling Facts

1. The first groups came to America
   □ a. to explore. □ b. to find gold. □ c. to worship.

2. People were not happy in their homelands because they could not
   □ a. vote. □ b. pay taxes. □ c. speak openly.

3. The Catholics settled in
   □ a. Virginia. □ b. Maryland. □ c. Connecticut.

4. The group that settled in Pennsylvania was known as
   □ a. the Quakers. □ b. the Mormons. □ c. the Pilgrims.

5. One common factor in all of the different religious groups was that the people
   □ a. used the same prayers.
   □ b. conducted the same service.
   □ c. believed in the same God.

Selection 46: Understanding Ideas

6. The article states that early groups of people in America
   □ a. suffered terribly during severe winters.
   □ b. were enemies of the Indians.
   □ c. helped one another to survive.

7. Early travelers to the shores of America were most impressed with
   □ a. the amount of open land.
   □ b. kinds of fruit they had never seen before.
   □ c. the number of trees for building houses.

8. The settlers protected themselves from their enemies with
   □ a. walls. □ b. guns. □ c. bows and arrows.

9. Most people came to America because
   □ a. they liked adventure.
   □ b. they wanted to become rich.
   □ c. they were unhappy at home.

10. The early settlers set up their own
    □ a. postal systems.
    □ b. welfare programs.
    □ c. governments.

47. AN APPLE A DAY

Apples have been grown by man since the dawn of history. They are often mentioned in early legends, poems and religious books. The fruit which the Bible says Adam and Eve ate in the Garden of Eden is believed to have been an apple. The ancient Greeks had a legend that a golden apple caused fighting among the gods and brought about the ruin of Troy. The Greek writer Theophrastus mentions a number of types grown in Greece in the fourth century B.C. Apple trees were grown and prized for their fruit by the people of ancient Rome.

The apple types from which our modern kinds developed had their beginnings in southwestern Asia in the area from the Caspian to the Black Sea. The Stone Age lake dwellers of central Europe used apples often. Remains found where they lived show that they stored apples fresh and also preserved them by cutting and drying them in the sun. The apple was brought to America by early European settlers.

The apple is more widely grown than any other fruit. It is considered the king of fruits. Apple trees of one kind or another grow all over the world. Only in the very hottest and coldest areas are they absent. Average apple production for the United States is about 6 billion pounds a year. Total world production is 26 billion pounds a year. Apple production in the United States and the world has been increasing and will continue to do so in the future.

Man, with his cleverness, has done much to improve the production of apples. The growing of apples has been a specialty with man for centuries. Greater improvements have been made in the last fifty years than in any other period of history.

The science of apple production has become difficult. In the past, scientists were mostly concerned with kinds, reproducing, and pruning. Today, the scientist working with tree fruits must also be trained in chemistry and plant forms.

Chemicals now play an important part in apple production. They are used to keep fruits free from disease and insect pests. Chemicals are used to thin or lower the number of fruits on a tree. They are used to control early fruit drop, cause flowering, control fruit size and improve fruit shape. When used properly, the chemicals are not a danger to human health. Without chemicals, very poor fruits would be grown.

Selection 47: Recalling Facts

1. The author mentions the Biblical story of
   ☐ a. Cain and Abel. ☐ b. Adam and Eve. ☐ c. David and Goliath.

2. The Greeks thought that a golden apple caused the destruction of
   ☐ a. Athens. ☐ b. Carthage. ☐ c. Troy.

3. Today's apple varieties are related to those that were grown in
   ☐ a. Europe. ☐ b. Asia. ☐ c. South America.

4. Annual apple production in the U.S. averages
   ☐ a. 6 billion pounds. ☐ b. 10 billion pounds. ☐ c. 18 billion pounds.

5. Apple production in the U.S. is
   ☐ a. increasing. ☐ b. decreasing. ☐ c. remaining constant.

Selection 47: Understanding Ideas

6. The author implies that
   ☐ a. many types of fruit are mentioned in the Bible.
   ☐ b. Europeans eat more apples than Americans do.
   ☐ c. primitive people preserved foods for winter months.

7. From the information presented, we can assume that
   ☐ a. apples are difficult to grow.
   ☐ b. apple trees grow best in cold climates.
   ☐ c. apples will not grow in extremely hot climates.

8. The article reveals that
   ☐ a. the U.S. is a major producer of apples.
   ☐ b. many countries do not grow apples.
   ☐ c. apples can prevent illness.

9. A farmer might reduce the number of apples on his trees so that
   ☐ a. apple prices will be kept high.
   ☐ b. apples will be larger.
   ☐ c. people will buy imported apples.

10. A person who wants to grow apples on a large scale should study
    ☐ a. history. ☐ b. chemistry. ☐ c. politics.

48. BRITISH TRADE

Trade is a way of life for the British. Britain ranks about seventy-fifth in size among the nations of the world. It ranks tenth in population but third in world trade. As one of the leading trading nations, it provides one-sixth of all the world's exports of manufactured goods.

However, the nation has few natural resources. There are supplies of coal and low-grade iron ore, but almost all other industrial raw materials must be bought overseas. Just over one-half of the food needed for the population can be grown on the limited amount of land.

Food and raw materials rank high on the import list of Britain. To pay for these imports, Britain must make and sell goods to the world's markets. Britain has worked long and hard to recover from the industrial damages of World War II and to regain its place in the world's markets.

Today there is hardly a country which does not have some form of trade with Britain. British cars travel the world's highways. Britain leads the world in the export of trucks and buses. Motorcycles are also a major export.

The shipyards of the United Kingdom have long been known for their work. Today they are turning out ships of all types and sizes.

Machinery of all types reaches the markets around the world in British ships. Radar sets, huge electrical generators, chemicals, and cloth of all types are also important export items. British-made leather goods, such as shoes and pocketbooks, are also sent to the world's markets.

More than 48 million acres of land in the United Kingdom are used for farming. Barley, wheat, oats and potatoes are the main crops of British farmers, who number only 3 percent of the working population. Their farms are among the best in Europe. They provide half of the nation's wheat and flour needs. They also provide three-quarters of the meat and cheese and nearly all of the milk and eggs that Britain needs.

Fishing is of special importance to Scotland since the great fishing banks of the North Sea are close at hand. Cod, haddock, and sole are caught in the deep waters. Herring, shellfish, and mackerel are caught in the shallow coastal waters. Canning and exporting fish to European markets is a large industry in Scotland.

Selection 48: Recalling Facts

1. According to the author, Great Britain has few
   - ☐ a. factories.
   - ☐ b. farming areas.
   - ☐ c. natural resources.

2. How much of its total food needs is Britain able to grow?
   - ☐ a. One-third
   - ☐ b. One-half
   - ☐ c. Two-thirds

3. Britain has worked long and hard to recover from the damages of
   - ☐ a. World War I.
   - ☐ b. World War II.
   - ☐ c. the Hundred Years' War.

4. Britain leads the world in the export of
   - ☐ a. grains.
   - ☐ b. steel.
   - ☐ c. trucks.

5. How many British workers are farmers?
   - ☐ a. 3 percent
   - ☐ b. 22 percent
   - ☐ c. 64 percent

Selection 48: Understanding Ideas

6. For the near future, it is unlikely that Britain will need to import
   - ☐ a. oil.
   - ☐ b. coal.
   - ☐ c. copper.

7. The author implies that
   - ☐ a. Scotland is part of Great Britain.
   - ☐ b. potatoes require a sandy soil.
   - ☐ c. the climate of Britain is cold and damp.

8. We can assume that the British do not suffer from shortages of
   - ☐ a. cotton and wool.
   - ☐ b. milk and eggs.
   - ☐ c. oranges and apples.

9. The article suggests that
   - ☐ a. gasoline is expensive in Britain.
   - ☐ b. most manufacturing is carried on in city areas.
   - ☐ c. land acreage is limited.

10. We can conclude that
    - ☐ a. Britain is a self-sufficient country.
    - ☐ b. Britain exports more than it imports.
    - ☐ c. Britain is greatly dependent on other countries.

49. A BACKYARD GARDEN

A backyard or some other space in full sunlight is the best spot for a home vegetable garden. However, poor drainage, shallow soil, and shade from buildings or trees may mean the garden must be located in an area farther from the house.

In planning a garden, one should think of what and how much to plant. It is better to have a small garden well kept than a large one full of weeds.

Many vegetables have colorful flowers. Some vegetables can be grown in a flower bed. Others can be grown entirely in containers.

The amount of sunlight a garden gets also is important. Leafy vegetables, for example, can be grown in some shade, but vegetables that produce fruit must be grown in direct sunlight.

The garden should be surrounded by a fence to keep out dogs, rabbits and other animals. The damage done by stray animals during a season or two can equal the cost of a fence. A fence also can serve as a trellis for beans, peas, tomatoes, and other crops that need support.

In most sections of the country, rodents damage garden crops. In the East, moles and mice cause much injury. Moles dig under the plants. They cause the soil to dry out around the roots. Mice either work alone or follow the holes made by moles. They destroy newly planted seeds and young plants. In the West, ground squirrels and prairie dogs damage vegetable gardens. Most of these pests can be stopped with traps.

Rich, deep, well-drained soil is necessary for a good garden. The soil should be well drained, well supplied with organic matter, and free of stones. The kind of subsoil is very important. Hard shale, rock ledges, gravel beds, or very deep sand under the surface soil will make the soil very poor. On the other hand, soil that has good qualities can be made rich. Using organic matter, lime, fertilizer, and other materials can improve it.

Good drainage of the soil is necessary. Soil drainage may often be improved by digging ditches and by plowing deep into the subsoil. The garden should be free of low places where water might stand after a heavy rain. Water from surrounding land should not drain into the garden. There should be no danger of flooding by overflow from nearby streams.

Selection 49: Recalling Facts

1. A garden should be located in
   - ☐ a. partial shade.
   - ☐ b. full shade.
   - ☐ c. full sunlight.

2. Vertical support must be provided for growing
   - ☐ a. peppers.
   - ☐ b. peas.
   - ☐ c. cucumbers.

3. Ground squirrels are often controlled with
   - ☐ a. poison.
   - ☐ b. traps.
   - ☐ c. fences.

4. What animal causes the roots of plants to dry out?
   - ☐ a. The mole
   - ☐ b. The chipmunk
   - ☐ c. The rabbit

5. According to the author, stones and rocks
   - ☐ a. retain moisture.
   - ☐ b. have no effect on a garden.
   - ☐ c. hinder plant growth.

Selection 49: Understanding Ideas

6. The author implies that
   - ☐ a. some vegetables have colorful blossoms.
   - ☐ b. most vegetables need a sandy soil.
   - ☐ c. a garden should not be planted near a building.

7. Green, leafy vegetables can be planted
   - ☐ a. along the bank of a stream.
   - ☐ b. in fertilized sandy soil.
   - ☐ c. in partial shade.

8. The author stresses the importance of
   - ☐ a. using organic fertilizer rather than commercial products.
   - ☐ b. digging the soil deep enough for good drainage.
   - ☐ c. covering the garden with straw during winter months.

9. Poor quality garden soil
   - ☐ a. can be used for flowers but not for vegetables.
   - ☐ b. can be improved with the use of lime.
   - ☐ c. can be mixed with gravel to improve texture.

10. We can conclude that
    - ☐ a. gardens which have good soil produce well.
    - ☐ b. most people think gardens require little work.
    - ☐ c. the most fertile gardens are found in the South.

50. DUE PROCESS OF LAW

There are many rights to make sure that people will be treated fairly when they are suspected or accused of a crime. Sometimes these rights are called "due process of law." In using these rights, a person should have the help of a lawyer.

You have a right against unreasonable searches and seizures. The police generally may not search you or your home, or take things you own, without a "warrant." A warrant is a paper which states, very exactly, the place to be searched and the things to be taken. Sometimes, however, the police will not need a warrant to search you or your property. If an officer sees you committing a crime, or if he has a good reason to believe you have committed a serious crime, he may arrest you and search you and the area right around you without a warrant.

If you invite a policeman without a warrant to come into your home and he finds proof of crime, the evidence may be used against you in court. If you do not want an officer to search you or your home and he does not have a warrant, tell him that you do not give him the right to search. However, if the officer will not listen, do not try to stop him. It is dangerous to resist and it may be illegal to do so. Any evidence which a policeman gets during an unlawful search and seizure cannot be used against you.

Police must act reasonably and fairly at all times. They should use physical force only when it is needed to arrest someone or enforce a law. Police may not use physical violence to "teach someone a lesson."

In all serious criminal cases you will get a lawyer free if you cannot afford one. You should ask for a lawyer as soon as you are arrested and when you are first brought before a judge.

No person can be forced to be a witness against himself. When in police custody, you do not have to answer questions which might help convict you of a crime. This means you may remain silent. You also may refuse to answer questions unless a lawyer is present. If you give information about a crime or confess to a crime because you were forced to do so, the information or statement cannot be used against you in court.

Selection 50: Recalling Facts

1. A person can legally refuse to testify against
   ☐ a. a relative.   ☐ b. a husband or wife.   ☐ c. himself.

2. For an officer to search you without a warrant he must have
   ☐ a. a judge's approval.   ☐ b. your permission.   ☐ c. court transcripts.

3. If you are arrested, you should ask first to see
   ☐ a. the evidence.   ☐ b. the warrant.   ☐ c. a lawyer.

4. You may remain silent when asked a question if you are
   ☐ a. in police custody.   ☐ b. in court.   ☐ c. before a judge.

5. A lawyer is provided if you cannot afford one in
   ☐ a. civil cases.   ☐ b. misdemeanor cases.   ☐ c. criminal cases.

Selection 50: Understanding Ideas

6. This selection could have been titled
   ☐ a. A Day in Court.
   ☐ b. Search Warrants.
   ☐ c. Rights of Citizens.

7. The selection shows that the author is in favor of
   ☐ a. court reform.
   ☐ b. due process of law.
   ☐ c. better pay for lawyers.

8. We can infer from this selection that
   ☐ a. laws also protect people accused of crimes.
   ☐ b. once caught, criminals usually cooperate with the police.
   ☐ c. the police often search homes without court approval.

9. According to this article, a "warrant" is
   ☐ a. a cruel deception.
   ☐ b. a legal document.
   ☐ c. a personal appeal.

10. This selection is meant to be
    ☐ a. humorous.
    ☐ b. sarcastic.
    ☐ c. informative.

PROGRESS GRAPH

Selection	26	27	28	29	30	31	32	33	34	35	36	37	38	39	40	41	42	43	44	45	46	47	48	49	50
Score																									

WORDS PER MINUTE

2400																									
800																									
480																									
345																									
265																									
220																									
185																									
160																									
140																									
125																									
115																									
105																									
95																									
89																									
83																									

TIME-RATE CONVERSIONS

Reading Time	Words per Minute	Reading Time	Words per Minute
:10	2400	2:40	150
:20	1200	2:50	140
:30	800	3:00	135
:40	600	3:10	125
:50	480	3:20	120
1:00	400	3:30	115
1:10	345	3:40	110
1:20	300	3:50	105
1:30	265	4:00	100
1:40	240	4:10	95
1:50	220	4:20	92
2:00	200	4:30	89
2:10	185	4:40	85
2:20	170	4:50	83
2:30	160	5:00	80